2012
THE BEST MEN'S STAGE
MONOLOGUES AND SCENES

2012
THE BEST MEN'S STAGE
MONOLOGUES AND SCENES

Edited and with a Foreword
by Lawrence Harbison

MONOLOGUE AUDITION SERIES

Smith and Kraus Publishers

ISBN: 1575257912
ISBN: 9781575257914
Library of Congress Control Number: 2164-2346

Typesetting and layout by Elizabeth E. Monteleone

A Smith and Kraus book
177 Lyme Road, Hanover, NH 03755
Editorial 603.643.6431 To Order 1.800.558.2846
www.smithandkraus.com

Printed in the United States of America

Contents

SCENES

FOREWORD

Here you will find a rich and varied selection of monologues and scenes for men from plays which were produced and/or published in the 2011-2012 theatrical season. Most are for younger performers (teens through 30s) but there are also some excellent pieces for older men as well. Some are comic (laughs), some are dramatic (generally, no laughs). Some are rather short, some are rather long. All represent the best in contemporary playwriting.

Several of the monologues are by playwrights whose work may be familiar to you, such as Don Nigro, Stephen Adly Guirgis, Jacquelyn Reingold, José Rivera, Adam Bock, JT Rogers, Adam Rapp, Carson Kreitzer, and Itamar Moses; others are by exciting up-and-comers such as Cassandra Lewis, Merridith Allen, Michael Mitnick, Chad Beckim, Thomas Higgins, and Katori Hall. The scenes are by veterans such as Don Nigro, Wendy MacLeod, JT Rogers and Greg Kotis, and exciting new writers such as Merridith Allen, Stephen Bittrich, Chad Beckim, Jussef El Guindi, Randall Colburn, and Jesse Eisenberg. Most of the plays from which these monologues have been culled have been published and, hence, are readily available either from the publisher/licensor or from a theatrical book store such as the Drama Book Shop in New York. A few plays may not be published for a while, in which case contact the author or his agent to request a copy of the entire text of the play which contains the monologue or scene which suits your fancy. Information on publishers/rights holders may be found in the Rights & Permissions section in the back of this anthology.

Break a leg in that audition! Knock 'em dead in class!

Lawrence Harbison
Brooklyn, NY

MONOLOGUES

4000 MILES

Amy Herzog

Dramatic
Leo, twenty-one

> *Leo is speaking to his 91-year-old grandmother, Vera. It's the middle of the night, and Vera has come upon Leo, who can't sleep. He finally tells his grandmother the story of the recent devastating loss he has sustained, after staying silent about it for weeks.*

LEO: So we were in Kansas, because—even though that was way out of the way we wanted to hit the center of the country, preferably around the fourth of July for maximum earnestness slash unacknowledged irony factor. The timing worked out so it was July 3rd and we were approaching Gypsum, our small town America of choice, one bar, one diner, seventeen churches or whatever. And we were going west to east, so, wind at our backs. The wind comes out of the south in the summer, but more like the southwest, so in a way going west to east was a pussy move on our parts, but we kind of wanted to do the opposite of the historical—like American is east to west, so we were going the opposite way, also we lived out west, so. It was more honest to start there.Western Kansas is like ass flat, the cliché, so you're basically just riding the wind and if you pedal even a little bit in a low gear you hit fifteen mph no problem. Fifteen mph is a slow speed in a car, but on a bike it's pretty good, it's pretty good. So it's morning and the sun's pretty low; between the low sun and the flat ride and the good wind it's the perfect time to take shadow pictures. That means you take a picture of your own shadow while you're riding, totally a staple of the cross country bike trip, gotta have the shadow picture, and with our huge packs and panniers we were gonna have especially dope shadow pictures. Micah thinks he's a really good photographer, he thinks he has talent, so he's doing a lot of bullshit with shutter speed and framing and what have you and we're both taking shadow pictures and we hear a truck coming behind us, or I hear it, I assume Micah does, I think he does because we both hug the shoulder a little bit, still taking our shadow shots, and the truck gets louder and closer and passes us and I see it's a Tyson truck full of fucking crates of screaming chickens packed together and there are feathers flying out of the truck bed like some kind of I don't know what kind of metaphor, and I scream up to Micah who did I mention was in front of me,—look at that fucking slave poultry! And he looks back at me, he has his left hand on his handlebar and his right hand still on his bullshit professional camera and he looks back at me and he's laughing and he starts to say something but the truck bed separates from the cab and flies backward and takes him off the road. Before the ambulance came this PR lady from Tyson came. I didn't realize I was still holding my camera. She was like,—I'm sorry sir, but I have to confiscate your camera. She has to yell it for me to hear her over all these maimed and freaked out birds. I was like—my best friend is under three thousand chickens. She was like,—I understand you're upset, but this will be easier for both of us if you just give me your camera now. I was like,—I couldn't get to him, he's buried under there, where is the fucking ambulance? And she was like—I'm going to ask you one more time—and I threw my camera on the ground.

(silence)

So what I don't have is these pictures from Wyoming, we did these stupid corny timer shots at the top of the Continental Divide, in front of the sign that says the altitude and all that shit, there was still snow up there in June. He caught a fish in Yellowstone, with his bare hands, he stood really still and reached in and . . . I had a picture of him holding up this fish longer than his head and neck. Oh and we dipped our back tires in the Pacific, that's another corny thing you do, because then you're supposed to dip your front tires in the Atlantic when you get there. Which I have not done yet, incidentally, don't know why. And I got a little video of him dipping his back tire and pretending to fall off this rock into the sea because he was a fucking clown, you know, he was a gifted physical comedian, he could have done that for real. And then there are all the pictures of him I don't remember taking, and maybe losing those is worse than losing the ones I do.

(silence)

It took them about forty five minutes to get him out, and the funny thing was he hadn't sustained any trauma to his head or anything but he had been face down in the mud with hundreds of pounds of weight on him and he had suffocated.

(silence)

So the part that everyone's pissed at me about is that after I filled out all the paperwork at the police station and called his mom and my mom I got back on my bike and kept riding.

About Spontaneous Combustion

Sherry Kramer

Seriocomic
Rob, twenties to early thirties

> *Rob is an ex-assistant DA, a fine, upstanding, and very frustrated young man. He is in love with Amalia, and she's in love with him, and that's why she won't sleep with him—because she's scared that if they touch, or even get too close, their love will explode into flames—they will spontaneously combust. This is a situation he can't seem to resolve. He tries to bring his considerable legal skills to bear on the problem, going down a list of possible suspects in this irrational fear Amalia has of loving him.*

ROB: Let's face facts, Amalia. If you're not afraid of me because of the way I look, it follows that you do not love me for the way I look. That's assuming a cause and effect relationship between love, fear, and spontaneous combustion. There's a certain beauty about being loved for your looks. A certain—certainty. If someone loves you for your looks, chances are they are not going to change their mind. How could they change their mind about your looks? You look the way you look. They either love you for it or they don't. And your looks are something you can be sure of, because—there they are, self evident fact, anybody can see them, you can see them too. The further beauty of this system is that if you loved me for my looks but there was this one particular part, or two parts, even, of my looks you didn't love—say these were the parts that frightened you—I could, without too much trouble, change them. If you loved me for my looks I'd be crazy not to. But if you don't love me for my looks I don't know where to start. There is limit, a range, a—certainty—to the sound of my voice, in the color of my eyes. If you loved me for that particular sound, that shade of color—I'd be safe, secure. But there's no telling what the rest of me—if it's the rest of me you love—can do. If it's something inside me—something I can never see and can never know, how will I identify it? How will I ever be able to make it go away? And if what has got you frightened is also what you love—then why should I?

Information on this playwright may be found at
www.smithandkraus.com. Click on the AUTHORS tab

About Spontaneous Combustion

Sherry Kramer

Seriocomic
Glen, middle fifties

> *Glen is a frightened man who has built an 18 hole golf course inside his home because the uncertainties of the weather keep him from playing outside. When his wife washes the dishes, she has an excellent view of him teeing off on the 16ᵗʰ. But at the moment he can't play the 7ᵗʰ—his daughter Amalia is in the bathtub, and she won't get out. She's terrified of spontaneous combustion, and she wants her boyfriend Rob to get in the tub and live in it with her. Glen sees it as his responsibility to talk Rob into getting into the tub. So he tells Rob a story about the day he gave up golfing outdoors for those he loved.*

GLEN: I was not always afraid of golfing, Rob. I was not afraid of golfing, before I was married. Why, did you know that Molly's mother and I met on the course? We went out together every Saturday. But then Mary Catherine was born. And just like that I felt the thrust of my life forcing me to live one long life insurance commercial every time I stepped on to a tee box. Other golfers terrified me, I had to let everyone of them play through, had to keep my eye on them all, making sure I never had my back to their wood shots. And the lightening. Suddenly the merest possibility of a storm sent me full throttle to the club house. My irons somersaulting off the back of the cart. And all to get home safe to Victoria, to Mary Catherine, and to my Molly. Once I . . . once I . . . I ran my cart over the 18th green. I was so desperate to get back to them. That was the last time I ever went out on the course.

Information on this playwright may be found at www.smithandkraus.com. Click on the AUTHORS tab

ADORATION OF THE OLD WOMAN

José Rivera

Dramatic
Cheo, thirty

> *Cheo is speaking to Vanessa. Vanessa is new to Puerto Rico and Cheo, in trying to romantically win her over, is also trying to seduce her into seeing the beauty of the island.*

CHEO: While you're in Puerto Rico, you should take a real good look around. Before it's too late. And don't do it with Izzy—he only knows what the tourists know. Promise me you'll do that? Because all this is gonna be gone some day. Little neighborhoods like Las Arenas, their little plots of land, full of chickens and pigs, this semi-independent way of life . . . it's all disappearing, like the coqui . . . getting buried . . . as the highways get closer. Even the stories told by old women like Doña Belen, the stories that hold these barrios together and connect the past with the present . . . all that's dying. There was a place I used to swim in, when I was a kid. On the beach, outside Arecibo, beautiful little bay called La Posa. It was my spot. Diving off the rocks. Time would stop for us. Black kids, white kids, we were one color: the color of fish. And the ocean was our home. The sun was our clock. Nobody was hungry in that water. Nobody was ignorant. I used to think . . . it must've been like this for the Tainos: perfect, pure, endless. One day I walked there . . . there's a fence. La Posa was bought by a U S hotel chain and the thing that was mine—and all us kids—was out of reach. For the fucking rich tourists. I hated that fence. Made my hands and feet bloody trying to do Kung-Fu on it. Begged Doña Belen to hit it with a curse. But La Posa died. When I stopped breaking my hands, I went home to think and I realized the only way out of this was nonviolent political action. That's all I've thought about. Now I'm a month away from finding out if I wasted my life.

AFTER

Chad Beckim

Dramatic
Monty, mid-thirties

Monty has recently been released from prison, where he spent 17 years for a crime (rape) he did not commit. He has been exonerated. Following news about the loss of his beloved dog, Monty voices his grief to Chap, his friend and former counselor. Laura Chapman is the woman who accused him, who has been trying to contact him since he was released.

MONTY: Ripley was a good dog, man. A good dog. No, a great fucking dog. The best. I taught her to sit. I taught her to stay. I taught her to lie down. I taught her to shake—even though I wasn't supposed to. I taught her to nudge someone's hand when they were scared or angry or anxious or just, just shut the fuck down. Me. I did that. The first night in that place with me, she cried. She fucking whined, man. Just scared. Cold and dark and metal and concrete and fucking . . . hell, man. Fucking hell. And because I was used to it, I had to make her okay. And I got down on the floor with her, on her bed, and laid down next to her, and I talked to her all night and stroked her head—that was her favorite—the top of her head—and took care of her. I made her not afraid. I made her okay. I did that. I got her through hell and I made something good happen. One good thing that I did. And now it's like everything else. Gone, man. It's all gone. You ask me what I have left? I have nothing.
(A long beat.)
Laura Chapman can suck my dick. Fuck that bitch, man. Fuck her. The state can suck my dick. $250,000? $10 mill? What's the fucking difference, man? I am seventeen years old. Seven-fucking-teen. I don't know how to tie a tie. I don't know how to shop for toothbrushes or deodorant or toilet paper. I don't know how to use a computer. I don't know how to kiss. My dick doesn't work. I can't help my

friend, I can't protect a woman. I cannot do anything anything ANYTHING without being told to. The only fucking good thing I ever did is gone, and you come here telling me that the good news is that they want to pay me for missing my prom and college and keg parties and my first apartment? Fuck them. Fuck the dude that killed my dog. And fuck Laura Chapman.

(A long beat. He turns to the window.)
Show yourself out, man.

After the Revolution

Amy Herzog

Dramatic
Ben Joseph, late forties-early fifties

> *Ben is leaving a message for his daughter Emma, who, having discovered that Ben withheld information from her about her beloved grandfather, is refusing to speak to him. Ben and Emma have always been extremely close, sharing values and ideals, so this breach in their relationship is deeply discomfiting to Ben. It is especially difficult because the argument centers around Ben's father, whom he idealizes and whose legacy he wishes to preserve.*

BEN: My question is are you not picking up your phone for anyone or did you get caller ID just to avoid me? Or are you screening? Are you listening to me, right now? Pick up the phone, Emma. This is your dad and you're hurting me a lot. Please pick up the phone.

(pause)

I was reelected president of the teachers' union this week. I know you think it's time I retired and let somebody young with new ideas step in, maybe a woman or somebody of color, but honey, nobody with any real vision came forward and there was a lot of pressure on me to run again so I caved and I did. This is the kind of thing I'd usually like to talk to you about, see if you think I did the right thing. Emma? If you're there? Please?

(Emma seems like she might pick up. Then, angrily.)

Okay, since this fucking machine is the only way to talk to you, let me tell you a few things you might not have thought of. When he first got involved in the spying, we're barely out of the depression, that meant thirty percent unemployment, it meant you don't walk past a garbage can without someone elbow deep in it. This is the landscape of my father's childhood and young adulthood. Now who are the people speaking up on behalf of the destitute? The American Communist Party.

Who is talking about racial equality, twenty—five years before the civil rights movement? Same answer. Who is calling attention to the fact that Russians are dying by the millions fighting fascism so that American hands can stay clean? Same answer, Emma. So who is my dad's allegiance to? Is it to J. Edgar Fucking Hoover? Is it to a president who fully intends to sell out the Soviets once Hitler is out of the way? No, it's to his party, it's to the honest working class Russians who are dying so that he can be free. So that his kids, and their kids, that's you, could be free. You want to condemn him from where you're sitting, kiddo, from your upper west side apartment, fine, but he's my father and I want nothing to do with it.

The Almond and the Seahorse

Kaite O'Reilly

Dramatic
Tom, late fifties

Thomas Williams is originally from Wales, but not a Welsh language-speaker. He is speaking through a locked door in a respite centre to his wife of thirty years, Gwennan, who has survived Traumatic Brain Injury from a car accident in late 80's. Thomas has been her care-giver for over a decade, but tonight he realizes fully she no longer recognizes him and is frightened by his presence.

TOM: I'm still here. Gwennan? It's me. Tom. Your husband, Tom. Thomas. Thomas Patrick Cleary, from the concert. Some concert thing or another, a recital, I didn't want to go. Fidgeting, rustling my program, my foot tapping the back of your chair. Sssh you said. Sssh. Sssh. I didn't know how to behave. They didn't go in for music in the dump I went to. It wasn't education, or not so you'd notice. Perhaps it was tough education like there's tough love, y'know, being taught things from the school of hard knocks? Well, love, I've certainly learned. Whatever lesson I was supposed to learn, I have it now by heart.
(to doctor)
In a minute.
(to Gwen)
So after the interval, you weren't sitting in front of me anymore, you were up on the stage, playing. And Gwennie, I'd never heard anything so beautiful before. And the next thing I know, I'm waiting for you after the concert, asking you out for the following Saturday and get this, and get this Gwennie—you said yes! Yes, to me, the dreamy no-hoper from the local tech, without one jot of music in his bones. I couldn't believe it. Nineteen years old and thought I'd won the lottery. So I took you to some movie—action-packed, boys' stuff, guns and hormones, I can't remember its name

now, didn't even watch it, just sat there in the dark watching the light from the screen flicker on your face. And that was it. Simple as that. Heart on the sleeve, ring on the finger, till death us do part. The end. So, Gwennan, Gwennie . . . So, now that we're reacquainted, will you open the door and let me in, please?

Information on this playwright may be found at
www.smithandkraus.com. Click on the AUTHORS tab

American Duet

Mark Leib

Dramatic
Charlie, twenty-three

> *Charlie is speaking to Jessica, the young woman he loves.*
> *Charlie, who was at first not political, has started working*
> *for the Jimmy Carter presidential campaign leading up to*
> *the election of 1976. He has chosen this path partly because*
> *of his own beliefs, but also because Jessica has indirectly*
> *informed him that she can't love a man who's not politically*
> *engaged. The fact that Jessica is married—and has told him*
> *outright that she's unavailable to him romantically—hasn't*
> *daunted him one bit.*

CHARLIE: Look, Andrea and I went to see *Rocky* a few days
ago. Have you seen it? Well, this is the story of a loser, a
nobody, a washed-out case who gets a shot at the heavyweight title, and a chance to redeem all the humiliations
he's suffered his entire life. And I'm sitting there in the
movie theater, and I'm thinking, I identify with him. Me,
from an upper-middle-class home, and I can't help but see
myself in Rocky Balboa. Because I was supposed to get
lost in the shuffle, just like him. My parents expected me
to become an attorney like every other kid I knew, and just
like them I was supposed to make an enormous amount of
money, and just like them I was supposed to stay high on
steak dinners and vacations to the South of France, and I
was to die a rich and happy nobody, totally detached from
any issue that mattered more than the relative comforts of
a Mercedes and a BMW. And I was moving along fine on
this pleasant trajectory, and I took one small detour: I fell
in love with you. And you said to me something, you said
you knew in your heart that one day I was going to involve
myself in the world. That I was going to notice it, the politics
and the history and the suffering too. And I made a start—I
wrote a thesis about an event that we both lived through

but that I really didn't understand. And then that wasn't enough, so I signed up with this campaign, which I just knew you'd approve. And now I don't know what's next, but I've taken steps, and I'm sure that others will follow. My life's going to matter, and not just to my stockbroker. That's what you've done to me.

Information on this playwright may be found at
www.smithandkraus.com. Click on the AUTHORS tab

American Lullaby

Cassandra Lewis

Dramatic
Tobias, thirty-five, a college professor. African American.

Tobias confronts Buddy, a retired Congressman (Caucasian, male, 67). They are in the Congressman's home, a southern plantation during a winter rainstorm. At first, Tobias appeared as a stranger stranded by the flood, but he has gradually revealed that the Congressman's ancestors enslaved his family and the plantation has housed both families for generations. Faith (Buddy's daughter, 38) has just admitted that she remembers holding a baby when she was a child and that it very well could have been Tobias, who was born there.

TOBIAS: That must have been the day my mother decided to leave, the day she chose freedom. It was a sad day because it was also the day my father died . . . You paid people next to nothing because working on this plantation was all they ever knew. Their parents and their parent's parents and so on worked on this plantation for generations. How would my grandmother and mother get any other job? It's all they knew . . . Don't disgrace my family any further by pretending you don't remember them. I have a letter right here *(pulls a folded note from his pocket)* from my mother that explains everything that you did to us . . . He cornered her like an animal and tore into her. He would creep into her bedroom, which of course was inside the old slave quarters. Cover the windows with new curtains and now instead of "slave quarters" it's a "guesthouse" for the poverty-level help. She was afraid of losing her job and not just her job, the Congressman had also threatened to fire and kill her mother too, Amerika Dupris, who as it turns out was raped by your grandfather until he finally died, also of a heart attack. Meanwhile your mother needed a farm-hand and my mother suggested she hire my father. When the Congressman found out my mother had suggested her husband move in and work here he beat her so badly she was in the hospital for two weeks and never got over the brain trauma that caused blinding migraines. She was so ashamed that she told my father that she was jumped by a gang. That's how bad the beating was. And that wasn't the end of the raping. Instead of creeping into her bedroom at night the Congressman would grab her as she tried to do her work—hanging the laundry on the clothesline, putting fresh sheets on the bed, probably even while changing your diaper. My father had his suspicions but didn't have the heart to ask until shortly after I was born. There was a question about who my real father was . . . For years, for all of my childhood I didn't know. I used to watch your father, the great American Congressman, on television and imagine all the ways I'd confront him someday. There he was making a holiday commemorating Confederate soldiers and installing a Confederate army memorial statue, spitting in the face of black Americans. It wasn't until a few years ago when I was able to get a DNA test when I finally knew where I stood in this world. I was able to let go of a lot of hate, but not all of it. My father died thinking he wasn't my father and now your father died thinking he was my father. Now that I am a father, I'm trying to understand just what exactly I'm supposed to do. All I know is the past is more important than I thought it was. You can't move forward until you own the past, for better or for worse. You can't reinvent history or pretend it never happened. Nothing will ever change until we learn that.

*Information on this playwright may be found at
www.smithandkraus.com. Click on the AUTHORS tab*

ASSISTANCE

Leslye Headland

Comic
Vince, late 20s

Vince works for a high-maintenance boss in a high stress job.
He has just been promoted from Assistant to Director and is
on his blue-tooth sharing the news with someone.

VINCE : PREEE-moted. Promoted. It's official. Director. Dee-
OR-rector. As of two weeks ago.
(pause)
Exactly. Absolutely. No kidding.
(pause)
Of course. OF COURSE! I know but we should talk about
that as soon as possible. I think so anyway. You're a good
person. So am I. We're great people and I love this and you
and the whole thing. I think it could totally work.
(pause)
I love the idea of him. Yes. Oh yeah. He could do it. He
could TOTALLY do it. He could do it. He could. We just
need to get him. See if he's available and then he'll do the
crap out of it. You know? Absolutely. I love this.
(pause)
No. I've got a landline, a business card, a cell phone, a
blackberry, a desk, don't have an assistant yet but I've got
an intern I just planted my flag in and you know what I mean
when I say that so . . . I've got a fucking home number that's
how reachable I am. I'm uber-reachable. You reach out.
I'm there. I'm here. I'm wherever it is that you need me.
Have someone send me every conceivable way of getting
in contact with you. I need that in my life right now.
(Laughs loud, hard and long. Too long. Awkward.)
That's what I'm saying! He could do it. I'll have my intern
find out if he's available. And when I say my intern, I mean
the assistant that I'm not paying. Best kind. School credit.
That intern humped my leg so much today that I thought
my pants were gonna catch fire.

(pause)

This is great. You're great. You look great. That's the most important thing. When it comes right down to it. Better to look good than feel good. You do! You look incredible. I wanted to fuck you so hard last time I saw you at the thing with the guy from that last project you kicked the shit out of. Fuck you so hard that when I came it would shoot out of your mouth. Jesus. JESUS! Jesus would fuck you that's how hot you are.

(pause)

Call me. E-mail me. Do whatever you gotta do. What are you doing tonight? Where are

(pause)

Text me when you get out. I'll be in the area so yeah . . . get on that. I wanna see you. Make it happen. Or I'll slice your stomach open and finger your liver. Chew on your small intestine. Got it. Yeah.

(pause)

From now on, don't say goodbye to me. Ever. Just hang up on me. That's what I want and need. Hang up. Just hang up.

(pause)

Hello? Hello?

(He ends the call. He types on his blackberry for a moment. Then he looks up and stares at nothing.)

Assistance

Leslye Headland

Seriocomic
Justin, twenties

> *Justin works for a demanding, high maintenance boss. Here*
> *he is on the phone with his therapist.*

JUSTIN: I'm fine . . . Yeah. No. I'm great . . . Thanks for doing
a session over the phone . . . I've been sick. So . . . but I'm
fine . . . Thank you . . . Sorry . . . Um . . . Yeah . . .
(pause)
Well, actually, I've been home for a few days. Out of the
office. I can't, sort of, go anywhere right now. My doctor
says I should rest . . . and I have stairs . . . Because walking is . . . has become an issue. Does that make sense? . . .
because . . . I broke my foot . . . Sorry I wasn't like . . . up
front with you about.. the foot thing . . . That's my bad.
(pause)
Yeah . . . I know I'm supposed to talk about these things
with you but I knew you'd say that and I know I'm not supposed to guess what your reaction is going to be because
then I lie about stuff . . . but you know, I don't really want
to hear it . . . Yeah . . . Sorry . . . I guess I pay you to say
that but I'm not even sure why I'm paying to hear shit I
don't want to hear because I don't have the money for this
therapy on top of the physical therapy I now need for my
foot. So . . . that's awesome.
(pause)
Yeah . . . Basically . . . I'm calling to break up with you. As
my therapist. I guess . . . Sorry. My insurance won't cover
the physical therapy or real therapy so . . . Gotta make
a sacrifice somewhere . . . Yeah . . . so that . . . sucks.
(pause)
Sure . . . totally . . . let's talk about it. I mean, I already paid
for this break up talk so . . . I was in London with Daniel.
We got off the plane. I went to get in the car. He had a con-

niption about the car. He got in the car. He told me to get in the car. I got in the car. We drove ten yards. He told me to get out of the car. I did. Then the driver sped off with Daniel. And the car ran over my foot.

(pause)

Yeah . . . I know. Ouch. Totally.

(pause)

Oh no no no no . . . Nnnnnnnoo. It wasn't Daniel's fault. It was my fault. I was standing too close to the car . . . Yeah . . . that was my bad . . . Sorry . . .

(pause)

No I mean . . . I get it. For sure. I know that. But, like, every job is "hazardous". In some way, right?

(pause)

But like . . . Stop! Okay . . . How is this is HIS fault? He wasn't driving the car . . . it was some gypsy or something . . . . He wasn't thinking about me. He wasn't doing it on purpose . . . He was just trying to get to the next place . . . you know? The next place . . . the hotel . . . and I was in the way . . . when I shouldn't't've been . . . I should've been helping and I wasn't helping . . .

(Pause. Justin laughs. Uncomfortable.)

I mean . . . Agh . . . I mean . . . . Give me a break . . . I mean . . . . This is totally why I'm breaking up with you. I don't need this. I don't need another person telling me to quit this job. If this job were easy, everyone would do it . . . STOP! I don't need another person telling me Daniel Weisinger is an asshole. If he acted like everyone else, he'd be everyone else. He'd be a nobody. He'd be YOU! So don't you DARE sit in your post-Freudian armchair and judge him when the whole world knows his name and you, you will die alone with only a vague satisfaction that you ate, shat and fucked your way to the grave never having seen greatness. I've seen greatness. I'm next to brilliance every day. And it needs to be defended constantly. He needs to be protected from nobodies LIKE YOU!

(long pause)

Sorry . . . Yeah . . . Sorry . . . Totally. I appreciate the advice . . . I'm not gonna take it because I don't need it . . . Sorry . . . Thank you . . .

(pause)

Because I take responsibility for my mistakes. And that's all this was. A mistake. My mistake and it won't happen again . . . . I don't need you. I need to get back to my job. Because he needs me.

(pause).

Okay . . . Great . . . Fuck you . . . Sorry . . .

(He hangs up. He stares at nothing.)

BLOOD AND GIFTS

J.T. Rogers

Dramatic
Simon Craig, late thirties

Simon, a British MI6 operative in Pakistan in the 1980's during the Soviet invasion of Afghanistan, is talking to his American counterpart in the CIA, giving him a heads-up about what is going on in Afghanistan.

SIMON: I was in Afghanistan about a month. Started in the Panjshir. From there, Kabul, Kandahar, then circled round, and crossed back over. Beautiful, hell; everything in between. Like everywhere else in this region, only with the world's largest army looting everything in sight because Moscow can't be bothered to feed her own soldiers. When I crossed back over here, I met with Hekmatyar.
(off Jim's look.)
Someone on our side needs to take his measure. Well for the devil himself he's rather disappointing at first. Bit of a fatty, really. Makes him look rather boyish. No warlord fashion sense whatsoever. Fatigues, scuffed boots, bushy beard: like an Islamist Castro. But then you look into his eyes and they chill the blood. Day after I left him I got word he'd ordered his men to start wading through the refugee camps, killing his own people because they're not pious enough. Christ, he's doing things almost as savage as the Russians. Do you know what they've started doing? Bayoneting children. No more "hearts and minds" for our dear Slavic friends. Oh, no. It's all napalm and landmines now. Corpses stacked so high the stench makes it hard to breath. And I tell you, Jim, I've had it up to here with those tea-sipping cunts back home who think the Soviets are the fucking Red Cross. As if the fate of the free world didn't hinge on us drawing a line in the sand and saying: "Here, and no further, you murdering Bolshevik bastards."

Charles Winn Speaks

C.S. Hanson

Dramatic
Charles, thirties

Charles, a Russian immigrant who has become wildly successful on Wall Street, speaks into a mini-cam, delivering a message to his wife, Jain, before they are about to go on a trip to Europe. This is his way of telling her he wants a divorce.

CHARLES: Before you. Another girl. But I did not see her. I let her be. And yet, I had a photograph. Her photo. For this you will hate me. I commissioned ten artists. To one, I say, "Paint her. What you see." To another, "Paint her sexy." To another: "Paint her as you would paint a monster." "Paint her as a nightmare." "Paint her lost in a forest." "Paint her as a last memory, the finest memory, an angel." I gave each artist 10 thousand cash. Same photo. To the street artists, it was a lot. To the commercial artists, it was just right. To one or two, it wasn't the money that mattered—it was the pursuit, the challenge. And now, now I have a storage room filled with paintings. I cannot bear to look at these paintings. I am ruining our life. You are crying. I have been in your place. I have been left behind. I remember, when it hit me, one night—after delivering a videotape—I cannot go into that—I made the driver hand it to her, as I crouched in the front seat of the SUV—does not matter—and I knew she . . . it's too hard to say. I knew it was over. I came home and went to bed and tried to sleep and that is when the large salty tears landed on my cheeks and rolled down my face. Like boyhood tears, but I was no longer a boy. I was supposed to be a man, but it hurt very much. For many nights, I would hold the book she left behind. Now, it is like I carry an invisible suitcase everywhere I go. Full of all the little moments with the girl. I'm sorry, Jain. I thought it was over. Try to forget me. Do whatever it takes. Forget. That is it. That is all. No. No. I want to say: Thank you, giraffe, for showing me the ocean and for driving a car with skill. And so fast, Jain, you are fast. Thank you for teaching me new words, like "bliss." I never used the word until I met you. I remember saying, "this is bliss." I remember how good it felt to buy you pretty things and watch you jump for joy. Joy . . . I am such a screw up. Call a lawyer . . . Go to Italy . . . . The reward? Easy. The apartment. It is yours.

Information on this playwright may be found at www.smithandkraus.com. Click on the AUTHORS tab

Charles Winn Speaks

C.S. Hanson

Dramatic
Charles, thirties

Charles, a Russian immigrant who became a Wall Street hot-shot, almost lost the woman of his dreams. In this monologue, which takes place in a hospital corridor, we realize he not only married the woman but she has just given birth to their first child. Speaking into a smart phone, Charles records a podcast to his newborn son.

CHARLES: This may be the only time I will get to say, I don't know, certain things. Once we leave this place, we'll be off and running. It will pass too fast. I want to hold on to time, to hold on to you. And so I make this podcast—for you and you alone. I speak to you while I can, before you are climbing the birch tree in our back yard and chasing . . . I get ahead of myself. Let me start with right now. You have all your toes and fingers. I counted. The nurse counted. I made the doctor count. The ears are good. The lungs are strong. I heard you cry. This is all good, very good. You are already getting an A. Little fellow. Boy. Son. I do not know what to say. You are my son. You will always be my son. I am your father. I will always be your father. You do not have a name. Your mother will pick the name. When she wakes. There is a list. There are five names on the list. I predict you will get one of the top three. If it were my decision, I would name you Roger. It's a good name. Roger. Roger. No one names their kid Roger. It is not even on the list. Your mother will decide. She knows best. For now, I will call you Roger. Roger, son, let me tell you about your mother. She is beautiful. In every way. You will see. When I first fell in love with your mother, she rejected me. I had lessons to learn and so did she—that is how she sums it up. It seemed our paths would never converge. But some years later—agonizing years—we got a second chance. I cannot explain. Roger, be brave. That's all I can say. Lessons. Math will be easy for you. And fun. Will it? It should be. English too. Do not be a selfish boor. I used to be a hot shot. Do not be a hot shot. I guess it's okay, if you are, but you're never as hot as you think you are. Do not change your name. Do not change it to Roger even though we both know it is a great name. Do whatever your mother tells you to do. It will be my responsibility to say no. "No, Roger, I said no." Once in a while I will say yes. For a whole day . . . on your birthday . . . every October the fifth, I will say yes all day long.

Information on this playwright may be found at
www.smithandkraus.com. Click on the AUTHORS tab

COMPLETENESS

Itamar Moses

Dramatic
Elliott, twenties

> *Elliott, a grad student in computer science, is taking to Molly,
> a molecular biology student with whom he may be in love,
> about his feelings about their relationship.*

ELLIOT: You know, I've been . . . coming to this computer
cluster, a lot, lately, just at random, different times of day,
just . . . Even though it's not remotely convenient for me, or
on my way anywhere, but just because I've been I guess . .
. hoping . . . And I know that I probably could have written
to you, or . . . called, I guess, but for some reason I felt like
I was supposed to just . . .
(beat)
Molly, I really like you? No, like, really a lot, and I'm at-
tracted to you, and you're really smart, and we're interested
in a lot of the same things, and I look forward to seeing
you, and I think about you when you're not around, and so
if I seem spare, or remote, well, then, I'm sorry that I seem
that way, but I promise it has nothing to with not wanting
to be close to you, or . . . wanting to be with other people,
or, okay, I mean, it does, of course it does, a little, I mean,
sure, I want to sleep with every attractive woman I meet,
or pass on the street, or am told about second hand, I mean,
you people don't know what it's like, you think you do,
and maybe you kind of do, in your way, but you don't, not
really, you do not . . . Not that I actually want to go out and
actually sleep with lots of people, that's an awful lot of
work, and it usually turns out to be more trouble than it's
worth, and, I'm getting off topic? What it is is: the fear that
actually knowing everything about each other will eliminate
the wanting. And so maybe what I was hoping was that, this
time, if I could hold something just close enough to keep
it from disappearing, but just far away enough to maintain

how I felt about it, which was good, by the way, this felt really really good, then maybe I could draw this first part out a little, because, I don't know about you? But I don't have any compelling evidence that something better after this? Even exists. That it ever gets any better than still wanting to be with you, and still knowing that I can, or ... could, because this obviously doesn't work either, does it, so ... Maybe, what's req ...

(beat)

I'm so tired. Of going back and forth. Between failing at this and wondering why I failed.

(beat)

I want us to know everything about each other. I want us to know so much about each other that it turns out we know less and less every day.

(beat)

Sorry. Too much? Too soon?

Information on this playwright may be found at
www.smithandkraus.com. Click on the AUTHORS tab

CQ/CX

Gabe McKinley

Dramatic
Hal Martin, fifties, an Alabaman and southerner through and through.

After an evening of celebrating the winning of a record seven Pulitzer prizes in journalism Hal, the executive editor of the New York Times, recalls the events of September eleventh and how they put out a newspaper that day. He speaks to his publisher, junior, and managing editor, Gerald.

HAL: Six days. It was the sixth day of my editorship and it was chaos . . . outside. But only outside. I walked through the lobby, and people were already gathering, some with photos of their loved ones . . . Thinking we could help. A woman grabbed my shoulder on the way in and asked me to help find her daughter . . . there was nothing I could say to her. Outside it was chaos. Inside, in the newsroom, it was this incredible quiet, so quiet it reminded me of a snow fall. That has always amazed me, that when things are the most chaotic . . . when major news breaks . . . a newsroom will become silent. Like a champion runners' heart that beats slow when the body is most taxed. By the time I got there we were already humming, a body at work, a living thing. Professional individuals working in concert . . . it was beautiful to behold. Employees walking from all over the city, dust in their hair, rushing to the office to work. They just wanted to work. Photographers and writers on the scene risking everything . . . to get the story. We knew about what everybody else knew, which is to say, nothing. Spotty phones and misinformation . . . but we put out a paper. We put out one hell of a paper. And every day after.
(beat)
I believe the papers produced during that period will stand the test of time. More importantly, we honored all those lives by bringing to our readers an accurate, balanced record of the crisis. A record.

(beat)

We all want to be remembered, don't we? Above all else. That's the most human thing—the want to be recorded, recalled—immortal. At the heart of it, we want to outlive death in the memory of those that come after.

(beat)

I'm proud the work we did. Not because of these awards we are celebrating tonight, far from. No. I'm proud that when the bell rang, we answered. That we *have always* answered when called to . . . and always will. A constant. We need to be, otherwise . . .

(Hal lights a cigar. He looks at the flame of his match or candle, at the light it gives.)

This is what we did. This is what we do. Illuminate the darkness . . . we shed light on the events of this world. A newspaper is a tool, a device, that shows us . . . what's out there. What we are, who we are . . . shows us what the world looks like. These awards, if nothing else, are a testament to that . . . a testament to all of us, but especially you and your family, Junior. Where would the city be without your paper? Without our "Portraits of Grief?" Where would America be without the New York Times?

(Hal raises a glass.)

Gentleman. To illumination . . .

DARKPOOL

Don Nigro

Dramatic
Dutch, thirty-seven

> *Dutch is a sort of mercenary, a veteran soldier of fortune who
> has probably worked for a number of shady organizations in
> and out of the government. At present he works for Darkpool
> Associates, a company which specializes in doing various
> sorts of dirty work overseas in support of government military
> activities. Dutch and his younger associate Mick have been
> called back to headquarters after a terrible incident in which
> something went wrong and a number of innocent civilians in
> an unnamed foreign country were slaughtered. Mick is very
> nervous about whether or not they're going to be tried for
> murder, and Dutch is trying to relax him by telling him stories
> about his past adventures. Dutch is tough, has a dark sense of
> humor, and is very likable. He is a decent fellow who makes
> a living doing indecent things.*

DUTCH: One time I was in this whore house in Serbia and
they sent over some character to kill me. The bad guys. So
they sent this guy to kill me. And this dude was as big as
a horse barn. I thought my ass was cooked. But there was
this little piano player in the whore house. I asked him to
play "Honeysuckle Rose," which has a sentimental value
to me because of my first wife. Now what are the odds I
find a piano player in a Serbian whore house who knows
"Honeysuckle Rose?" That little feller could play the hell
out of that song. So this big, dead-eyed, barn-sized turd
walks in. I had taken my gun off, which I do not recom-
mend, but the girl had a rule about that, and I'm a sucker for
redheads. Everybody's got a weakness. Maybe she was in on
it with him, I don't know. So anyway, this big goddamned
freak of nature comes in, looking like Lurch the butler in
the Addams family, and I figure I'm a goner. But just as the
guy pulls out his gun, the little piano player, who this guy

walked right past like he's a potted plant, picks up a pool cue and wallops Lurch in the back of the head, wham, and guy is stunned. He's on his knees. And then the piano player whacks him again, wham, right on the crown of his head, and the big guy falls face down on the floor and then kind of rolls half way over onto his back, and the little piano player takes that pool cue in both hands, and rams it right into the guy's throat, like he's digging a post hole, and the guy's artery erupts like Mount Vesuvius. He's sprawled out on the floor with this pool cue stuck in his neck, and this naked Serbian whore is bouncing off the walls, covered with blood, screaming bloody murder. It was a Kodak moment, let me tell you. So I want to give the piano player some cash, to thank him, but he says, no cash, give me job instead. Turned out he was an enterprising little fucker. So I said, what the hell, this guy appears to have the right disposition for this sort of work, so I turn him over to my buddy Popeye. Do you know Popeye? Before your time. And it turns out the kid has got a natural talent. He's moving right up the ladder. Then one day Popeye comes to me and says, Dutch, we got to get rid of this piano player. And I say, but Popeye, I thought the kid had a natural talent. And Popeye says, yeah, he's got talent, all right. The son of a bitch is fucking my wife. And I say to him, Popeye, I don't care if he's fucking the Queen Mother, this guy is a keeper. I mean, you need somebody to cut up a corpse, and this little Serbian piano playing fucker don't even blink. He did it like he really knew what he was doing. He said his uncle put him to work in the slaughterhouse when he was twelve, and once you've done that, nothing bothers you. You just turn off a little switch in your head. Of course, a couple months later, we did have to get rid of him. Turns out he was also fucking the boss's sixteen year old daughter. But he knew too much to fire, so we sent him out on one of those snipe hunts where you don't come back. We didn't have him killed. We just notified some of the more hostile locals of the location where he might happen to be hunting snipe. The moral of that story is, shoot the piano player first.

DARKPOOL

Don Nigro

Dramatic
Max, fifty-three

Max is the head of a large corporation which specializes in supporting shady government activities during military actions in foreign countries. He has his own private army and big plans for the future. Two of his operatives, the veteran Dutch and the younger Mick, have been called back to headquarters after a terrible incident in which a number of innocent people were slaughtered overseas. The situation is fluid, and at the moment it's possible they could be tried for murder, or perhaps Max's connections in the government will be able to get them off. What's critical now is damage control, and putting the right spin on their version of events. Max is giving Dutch and Mick a kind of pep talk, sharing his world view with them to help them see why they should behave the way he wants them to if they know what's good for them. Max is like a combination television preacher and motivational speaker for Rotary Clubs. He is very confident, brilliant, highly energized, engaging, very persuasive, and has a dark sense of humor. He would be very good at selling used cars, would make a great presidential candidate, and behind that big smile is probably dangerously insane.

MAX: So, we've got a little problem here we need to address. I've asked Justine to sit in because she's going to be taking the point on public relations in this matter and help represent you in court if it should come to that. But I don't personally think it's going to come to that. Not if we play this thing right. But don't worry about it, because one way or another, we're going to take care of you. Because here's the thing you need to understand about working for us. We're like a family here. And not just any family. We're God's family. And I say this not to puff myself up, but because I know it to be the honest truth, that those of us here at Darkpool are the direct instruments of God's handiwork. Which means we have a special dispensation to take whatever measures might become necessary, like the Crusaders of olden times. Because, make no mistake about it, this is a great Crusade we are engaged in here, my friends. And God's people are rewarded in Heaven, but also on earth, not just with money and power, but with all the fruits of the Garden. Look. Let's talk turkey. We are not children here. We need to put away childish things. I'm not going to insult you by offering up a plate of horse shit and apple sauce. This is how it is. You have an elected government to keep the people satisfied. This is absolutely necessary, and representative democracy is a great institution, as far as it goes. But it's largely an illusion. The real government is something else. The real government is us. You have a military to fight and die for our freedom, and I humbly honor these brave men and women every day of my life, in my prayers and in my aspirations. But in the larger geopolitical and macro-economic picture, what are they, really? Cannon fodder. Unfortunate, but true. The real military is us. For us, there are no laws but God's laws, because we're God's people, and we're pursuing a higher calling here. And I take this responsibility very seriously. Do you accept Jesus Christ Almighty as your Lord and Savior? Because I believe that when Jesus comes again, and trust me, he's coming soon, this time he'll be packing automatic weapons. No more of this turn the other cheek shit. He's going to be hunting moose and heretics from a helicopter. He's going to be one of us. So you guys got nothing to worry about. Believe me. I know. I grew up in the swamp. You can learn a lot in a swamp. God lives in the swamp. God is everywhere, but especially in the swamp. You can smell him best in the swamp. He lives under the water there. He's like a big crocodile. Ancient. Waiting.

Don Giovanni

Don Nigro

Seriocomic
Casanova, eighties

*Thrown into prison for his immoral escapades, the infamous
seducer Don Giovanni discovers his hero, Casanova, is also
a prisoner there. But to his horror he sees that Casanova is
very old, greatly decayed, and has false teeth that will soon
be knocked out—a terrible vision of what the middle aged
Don Giovanni is soon to become. Don Giovanni's servant,
Leporello, frustrated because the girls always want his boss
and never him, has just asked Casanova to give him some
advice on how he might attract women. As wretched and en-
feebled as Casanova has become in his old age, he absolutely
lights up when speaking about women.*

CASANOVA: Well, if I were you, I'd work mostly in the dark.
But you know, part of the secret, part of what men often
don't understand, is that, if they are unsuccessful with
women, it's not because women fail to appreciate them,
it's because they have failed to fully appreciate women.
One must never, ever, underestimate a woman, or take a
woman for granted. Any woman. We are fortunate to have
the honor of breathing the same air that women breathe.
There is no ecstasy on earth that compares even remotely
to the close proximity of a woman. Just to smell her hair, to
touch her flesh, the curve of her back, the shape of her lips,
her ears, her arms and elbows and hands. It is easy enough
to mock a man who praises a woman's elbow, but let me
tell you, there is no part of a woman which is not beautiful,
and there is nothing more intriguing about a woman than
the labyrinth inside her head. Everything about a woman
is intoxicating. It doesn't matter how old or ugly you are.
If in your heart you are a man who is intelligent enough
to truly appreciate a woman for her own sake, separate

from all else, separate from any vain and foolish desire to possess or control her, just to cherish each miraculous individual woman for herself, her own particular beauty, her own unique and irreplaceable soul, this is the greatest of God's gifts to us. When everything else is gone, at my very last breath, the last thing I will see in my mind's eye, the last image I will cherish, is the astonishing gift of even once in my life having been granted the tender love and intimate trust of a woman. There is nothing else that matters on this earth.

Don Giovanni

Don Nigro

Comic
Don Giovanni, late fifties

The aging Don Giovanni has inadvertently murdered Donna Anna's father, the Commendatore, causing her to fall into a despair that is close to madness. She won't eat. She can't sleep. She just sits brooding, wasting away, waiting to die. Although more careless by nature than cruel, Don Giovanni has always been extremely selfish in his relations with women, convincing himself that they want to be seduced by him, and that he is only performing a public service by sleeping with them. But now, observing the terrible consequences of his behavior, for the first time in his life he's become uneasy about what happens to the women he seduces and abandons. Here he is trying to cheer up Donna Anna and get her to eat and to live. Increasingly horrified at the consequences of his actions, he is slowly learning, with some astonishment, and probably too late, what it is to care more about another person's welfare than one's own. Donna Anna has just told him, in effect, that she doesn't want to live, and feels responsible for her father's death because she was bored, wanted to have adventures, and found it exciting to have a man in a mask crawl up the trellis onto her balcony and into her bedroom.

DON GIOVANNI: Look here. That's foolish. You didn't kill your father. Of course you were bored. Of course you were tired of being locked up in your room like a monkey at the zoo. Of course you wanted something to happen. You're young and beautiful and should have been out enjoying life. It wasn't wrong to want these things. It wasn't wrong to be excited and happy that somebody had finally cared enough to climb up your trellis, straining his lower back and getting horrible thorns in his palms just to get to you, to risk his life just to see you, to be near you, to smell the perfume of your hair, to gaze into your eyes. That wasn't wrong. That's just being human. What was wrong was for anybody to think he had the right to lock you up and keep you all to himself. A woman is not anybody's property. A woman is not anybody's slave. A woman is a free human being. She has rights just like anybody else. What happened to your father was his own doing. He tried to imprison you, and it led to his death. It was his fault, not yours. That man in the mask came to free you. And now, you're free. You're young. You're beautiful. You're rich. You have nobody to tell you what to do. The world is yours. You can live your life now. So get out of that rocking chair and put on a naked puppet show.

First Day of School

Billy Aronson

Seriocomic
Peter, thirty to fifty

> *Peter is a married parent. After dropping off his daughter for
> her first day of school, he runs into Susan, another married
> parent. In the middle of a conversation about which teach-
> ers their children have, Susan asks Peter if he would like to
> have sex with her. In this monologue, he attempts to answer
> her question.*

PETER: Hey I really appreciate what you said before, about,
you know. It's just, I can't. It's a question of, you know. But
I appreciate it. I really do. I think you're a terrific person.
I admire your spirit, and your friendliness, and your eyes,
they're just wonderful. You're a very wonderful person and
that means so much nowadays. It's just the old thing that
we live under. And I'm not saying it's bad, what you were
suggesting, it's completely natural. I just couldn't handle,
you know, the lying or whatever, Maxine and I tell each
other everything, well not everything, if there's a surprise
party for her obviously I don't tell her that but that's obviously different, or when I went out to get her those little
thingies that she wanted, the earrings, I told her I was going
out with this friend of mine Rob and that was a lie, let's call
it what it was it was a lie so we do lie and that's fine, she
completely accepts that we lie, everyone does in a sense,
but to be carrying around a secret, a big big secret, like
when she introduced me to this friend of hers she didn't
tell me that they'd slept together in college until after like
the fourth time we saw him so there I was socializing with
this guy who she'd gone out with in college, or it was high
school, Sasha was his name, Sasha Mallone, she'd totally
concealed their past because she knew it would make me
uncomfortable, she had this secret but so what. Yes we're
married, we're married but we have thoughts, I don't know

what she's thinking, we can't tell every thought, we're individuals, right? We have a bond, but we still you know, we have separate brains and separate lungs, we're not Siamese twins, we need to breath on our own like that time she gave my brother a massage, right in front of the fireplace, she goes right over to my brother, gives him a massage, I'm sitting there adding kindling like an idiot, nobody's massaging me but she massages him, and I was happy for them both, but I guess I know this thing you're talking about would be different, it's more, you know, what's the word, I can't think of the word, but it's definitely different and I'm only sorry because it'll mean I won't have a chance to get to know you in that way and it really limits, doesn't it, the way we can know each other, it's a shame that a budding friendship should be cut off like that and yes sometimes a friendship does sort of veer from one category into another and then it veers right back again, it swerves kind of, so we might have had a wonderfully swerving friendship and to just cut it off, to limit the possibility for joy in our limited time on earth, it seems a damn shame to cut off an opportunity like that, it's pathetic, that's all, to butcher a blossoming friendship with someone so obviously warm and outgoing with such beautiful arms and a smile and great hair and a great smell I mean why can't I just put my face in your hair and sniff it, you know? Why am I stuck standing here on the other side of some invisible divide, this boundary, where is it? Is it here, is it here? This ridiculous wall that separates me from someone with such honesty and openness and the courage to be direct, such guts, such heart, such warmth, why do we have to limit ourselves like that? What's the purpose? What's the logic, it's not logical. We're animals. We live. We have arms. So what.

Information on this playwright may be found at
www.smithandkraus.com. Click on the AUTHORS tab

Flesh and the Desert

Carson Kreitzer

Dramatic
Siegfried, age indeterminate. fifties-sixties

Siegfried is speaking to his partner, Roy. Roy has been mauled by a tiger during their act, and now lies in a hospital bed, unconscious after surgery, completely hidden beneath sheets.

SIEGFRIED: You remember that first time, you came to see my act? On that crazy cruise ship? And I made . . . what? A rabbit. Must have been a rabbit. Made a rabbit disappear. And you talked to me after. You said, "Could you do that with a panther?" Fifteen years old, in your little busboy uniform, black hair and brass buttons. And the smile. Oh, the ladies loved you. Ordering drinks to their staterooms, just to have you bring. And we stopped at ports, maybe three ports later, four ports later. And you came to me smiling. And you brought me to your tiny cabin, so small we could almost not stand up in it. You open the door and there he is—a leopard. I have never seen a leopard before, and here he is in your cabin. You . . . stole him from the zoo. Made him want to come with you. I still don't know how you . . .
(soft)
Yes. I do. You make people . . . want to follow you anywhere. That crazy smile, like the world . . . will always be beautiful, wherever you go. They put us off at the next port. Two boys and a leopard. And we . . . we made a pretty good job of it, yes?
(soft, leaning forward)
Please, please I know you can hear me. You can hear me. You're going to be—please. If you can hear me, just just squeeze my hand. Just a little bit.
I know it's hard. Please. Just try.
I know you can hear me. I know.

Hurt Village

Katori Hall

Comic
Skillet, late teens to early twenties, African-American.

Skillet tells Ebony, the neighborhood comedian and small-time doughboy, about a money-making plan he's come up with. He speaks very slowly.

SKILLET: You know how weed make you forget; I forgot. Speakina' which, I forgot to tell you. This niggah down by the Pyramid gone axe me, which one I rather have. Pussy or weed? I say, "Niggah? Now what kind of question is that?" I'm the type a niggah, can't live without neither, but I much rather have some weed than some pussy. Pussy and weed . . . got some similarities. Pussy and weed taste good when they wet. they both . . . got a distinct smell. They both can have you happy and give you the munchies til six o'clock in the morning. They both can burn ya' if you get too close to the tip. They both can turn yo' lips black, you suck on it too much. See, I likes em' both, but pussy leave you. Weed don't care nothin' 'bout yo' job, yo' credit or yo' car. Weed'll chill witcha . . . anywhere and nowhere. Make everything real . . . slow . . . motion like. Pussy speed shit up: the decreasement of the gas in yo tank, yo' bank account, and yo . . . beloved weed. Hell muthafuckin yeah! That's my next 'speriment. I can make pussy-smellin' weed! I'm on a marketing grind: "Pussy weed." Niggahs'll eat that shit up, you know what I'm sayin'? "Gotta make that money, cuz I gotta get my own place Can't stay wit' my cousin no mo. Gotta go. Gotta go I stay high on the ya-yo. Jump the boogie Woulja puff puff pass that pussy to me." That was brilliant. I'ma have ta record that Triple Six Mafia could use that verse.

Hurt Village

Katori Hall

Dramatic
Tony C., late thirties-early forties, African-American.

Tony C, the "Kang" of the Doughboys, controls the crack houses in Hurt Village, a poor community in the South. He is justifying his life to Cookie, a 13 year-old wannabe rapper girl who is looking for a way out.

TONY C.: The city know they stay pullin' that shit. Learn this befo' you learn anythan' else. Crackers ain't gone give you shit. You gots to take it. That's one thang niggahs ain't never learnt, yet. Not stealin', but takin'. Like we got a niggah mayor right—muthafuckin' Mayor Willie Herenton, right. But it's all fo' show cause that niggah don't care nothin' bout you or me. He gettin boocoo bank from the guvment to "revitalize" these here projects. Millions! Movin' niggahs out like Hebrews to make room for who? Crackers! City use the guvment money to bulldoze this shit, then these private developers gone swoop in like roaches to rice. Property value done dropped so they gettin prime muthafuckin' real estate for free. End of the day lil' Willlie rakin' in millions and then gone get paid more on the back end from these developer dudes. He too busy gettin' his dough, his paper. It's a muthafuckin' conspiracy up in this bitch cause you know they just gone build some condos up in this bitch. Hurt Village niggahs can't 'ford that shit. But thass the politickin' of the projects, pure and simple. Getcho shit together, you gotsta always be on yo' job. See these Chink ass mofos they got liquo stoes and check cashin' stoes takin 20 dollars out cho' check to give you yo' money. What kinda sense that make? What we got? Nathan! They make the money and take that shit out to wherever they at. We all gettin' fucked in the ass over here, niece. We all gettin' raped, but you got to get in where you fit in. Hell, I know my place. I sell that white to these niggahs so my lil' boy won't ever have to play on a playground got mo' crack vials than blades of grass. I'll be damned that happen. I'll be damned. So . . . if I gotsta kill a couple niggahs who was on they way out anyway, so be it. It's for the greater good.

I COULD NEVER LIVE HERE

C.S. Hanson

Dramatic
Johnny, mid-to-late forties

Johnny speaks to his sister Audrey, in the living room of the farmhouse in North Dakota, where they grew up. It is 1984. Johnny is dead, was buried yesterday, and now his ghost haunts his sister who came for the funeral and decided to sell the farm to save her marriage. Audrey's husband has stormed out, leaving her for good. Johnny, a painter who got stuck on the farm, wants Audrey to do the right thing.

JOHNNY: Now you know how it feels . . . to be left behind. No soft landings when a lover takes off. Grief is an isolating thing. Can't blame you for going under the covers. You want to go after him? What'll that prove? Won't prove love. If what you're feeling is love (and it probably is) it'll always be there, like a penny in your back pocket. Fine, have it your way, go after him. Keys are in the ignition, but that ol' pick-up won't go over forty-five without a battle. We're not followers. I was too stubborn to follow a woman who was so audacious as to take my child. We're cut from the same cloth, sister. No wonder we're screwed. Products of a mixed marriage: Norwegian and Swede, held together with stoicism and guilt when you're having fun. You want to ask: "How'd you do it, Johnny? How'd you stay here all these years?" I painted, just to bring some color into this frozen landscape. This is a good place as any for grieving. Something about watching a growing season that gives you hope. A farm is kind of like a piece of art. It's not obvious. You look out the window and think, when did those stalks of wheat get that tall? You're painting and you can't see what you have until you step away. No crop is like the one before it. Start a new painting, no idea if it's going to turn out. In ten minutes a hail storm can destroy a crop that's been growing for three months. In two minutes, after painting for two weeks, I could pick up the canvas, open the window in that studio, throw it outside, run down the stairs, go out and grab a fistful of mud and throw it on the picture. Don't think I haven't done that. Selling the farm, it's one of the hardest decisions a person . . . someone's gotta do it sometime. Do it when the time is right, Audrey, but not before. When you know in your heart it's time, then light the lamps and torch the place . . . Sleep, sister, for tomorrow's a big day. Tomorrow you'll take stock of your new . . . situation. I think it's already tomorrow, isn't it?

Information on this playwright may be found at www.smithandkraus.com. Click on the AUTHORS tab

I Know

Jacquelyn Reingold

Comic
Daniel, seventies (although an actor of any age could do just this monologue)

Daniel, a character actor, comes home to his New York apartment, knowing that Lila, his partner for forty years, has been diagnosed with a fatal illness. She doesn't know that he knows, and he doesn't want to let on. He is planning to propose marriage to her, tonight, after dinner.

DANIEL: Hello Darling—happy to see you—I missed you—you look beautiful as always—no—more beautiful, though how that is even possible I cannot imagine. How are you? *(no response)* Well, I had a helluvan actor's nightmare of a day, so to make things a little worse, I went shopping at Fairway. Remember when it was just a store with good produce, and all you had to fear were the crazy ladies with their carts? Now it has its own zip code, and every time I go, everything's been moved, so it makes even less sense then the no sense it used to make. I think they hired Paul Bremmer: he'd been unemployed since ruining Iraq, so they brought him in to create chaos at Fairway. You hungry? I thought I'd make a special 'Daniel Raskin' dinner. With back rub for dessert.
(no response)
How bout a drink? I know I could use one. You wouldn't believe the audition I had: some God-awful movie about Libyan terrorists living in an air pocket below the Hudson, who, when discovered by outer space aliens mate to create Mutant Terrorists poised to take over the world, and I, if cast, would have the memorable pleasure of playing a night watchman who utters the very important words "What are you doing here?" then gets killed by the Aliens' plutonium shooting third arm—for scale. So I went to my agent's office to suggest I not be submitted for such garbage, and,

between phone calls, he told me that all the casting directors who say I'm a pain in the ass are wrong, which, of course, was his way of telling me what he really thinks of me, without actually saying it. He did, however, mention five or six times, that if you were interested in changing your theatrical representation, since everyone loves you, he'd be thrilled to take you on and steal your ten percent. So my dearest and amazing woman, here's to you, because above all else, no matter what happens, and how awful it is or might be, I adore you. As I enter the lobby, slip past our sleeping doorman, I'm filled with anticipatory delight, and when I step into the elevator, it's not the only thing that albeit, slowly, starts going up. How are you? What did you do today? Tell me everything.

(no answer)

What's going on? Is it monologue night?

The Invitation

Brian Parks

Dramatic
David, fifty to sixties

*David is a book editor. This is David's impassioned sugges-
tion for how his wife Marian should be buried, after he has
murdered her at the dinner party. He is speaking to three
dinner guests.*

DAVID: Go! Go bury her!
(DAVID turns, inspired.)
No! Let's build her a mausoleum instead. No dirty grave for
Marian. No urn of overindulged ashes. A mausoleum high
on a hilltop, a final temple to herself! Build the walls out off
HD TVs and Bibles and million-threadcount sheets. Fake
Old-World landscapes and Burbury scarves. Faberge eggs,
wood chopped from rain forests, sables washed of blood in
Chinese sweatshops. Paper the walls with stock certificates
and condescending notes to housecleaners! Hammer it all
together with the skull of a smothered gold-miner. Then
build a roof! From dinner gowns and hunks of veal and
chinchilla hand muffs. Caulk it all with fois gras. Varnish
up the floor up with the blood of every Shawnee who died
to make her life beautiful. Drag in her ruby-and-risotto-
crusted coffin. Let the rented pallbearers say a quick prayer
from the Book of Common Avarice, then run for their lives,
locking the big stainless-steel door behind them! Take the
key and climb the nearest volcano and hurl it down into the
roiling lava pit—so that it sinks slowly down to Hell and
melts forever into Beezelbub's forehead!

*Information on this playwright may be found at
www.smithandkraus.com. Click on the AUTHORS tab*

Jerome Via Satellite

Jerrod Bogard

Dramatic
Dan Dillinger, forties

Once a scrappy journalist, Dillinger now hosts "The Spin Cycle with Dan Dillinger," a news-entertainment show like the O'Reilly Factor. He's bombastic and full of himself. On the 4th of July broadcast of "The Spin Cycle," a live videoconference between a U.S. soldier in Iraq and his family in Texas goes very wrong. They cut the live feed and go to commercial. During the break Dillinger confides to a prying makeup girl about his recurring dream.

DAN DILLINGER: I'm at a press conference in a grand ballroom. But it's actually a forest. You know how that is in dreams?—I see this on a blog and it's your ass . . . And I'm there and I'm surrounded by newsmen with microphones— but they're really aborigines with spears, poison tips, all pointed at my throat. Then this bell rings like the old movie studio bell, or like in high school and I'm hit with a flood of light. The natives are gone but now zap—I'm stuck—glued to this little X on the floor. I look up. And I'm frozen there under these unbearable hot white lamps. I'm literally a deer in the headlights now because now I'm this giant buck. This great, badass and beautiful buck I am, with just this mythic, 24 point rack. It winds up—twining up like the roots of an ancient oak. I'm posed before a setting sun, gorgeous so my silhouette is rimmed with this golden glow. And I have these cavernous nostrils—these two immense black holes to suck to flare these tremendous
(deep inhale)
surging breaths. And now I—as this beast—I look up and I see this red dot. Just this tiny red dot. A little red light that tells me God is watching. And it shoots me. Every night it shoots me. I'm venison. Seasoned to taste and served over conversation . . . .

(out of the dream now)

Now here I happen along here—Here we stumble by this screaming truth like a goddamn I.E.D.— a goddamn road-side bomb of human courage and frailty here, and I see that I'm not really sleeping at all. Or rather that I am not the dreamer. I'm—I'm the dream. I'm the dream because I make sense out of nonsense, and like a dream, pull narrative from the random. I make plain the extraordinary, and amazing just the plain ol' same ol' plain ol' same. And see, as long as you don't change the channel, I can keep you sleeping soundly . . . so that there's nothing to remember.

Just Your Average G.I. Joe

Jerrod Bogard

Dramatic
Joe, twenties

> *Joe is a family man and a professional soldier specializing*
> *in targeting for laser guided weapons, recently back from the*
> *Iraq War. He is having a beer by himself when a couple of*
> *guys buy him a drink and thank him for his military service.*
> *He reluctantly gets to talking, and soon finds that he can't*
> *stop, that he needs to share these things. Here he rationalizes*
> *his war-time deeds and reveals perhaps a little more than he*
> *had planned.*

JOE: If I wasn't good at it I wouldn't be doin' it. That's for
sure. Professional. That's the word. Man, I been in some
operations I'm not supposed to talk about. And I won't.
But the stuff that I can talk about—some of it's worse than
the stuff I can't talk about. I don't mean worse like worse,
like it's bad. It's just—shit gets scary sometimes. But when
it does, I aint thinkin' about yellow ribbons. I'm thinkin'
about how do I be professional. Most times bein' a professional means takin' a mother out before he takes any of us
out. You trust the intel, you do your job best you can. And
there's no second-guessing. Can't. You hesitate, people get
hurt. Pause, people die. That's the deal. It's exciting. Now
a lotta guys won't talk to you like I am. Some guys, my
best friend is like this, won't talk about it. They saw some
bad situations. Me? I'm alright so far. But that's—that's
just part of the thing.
(the following slowly builds in intensity)
One thing you gotta realize is: I don't miss. News says a
school caught a bunker buster- wasn't me or my guys. Was
the intel. Far as I know, I never hit a school and I never
hit a hospital. Not once. Nobody does. We hit targets. We
get the target. We paint the target. We take the target out.
Do you think they'd tell us if we hit a hospital? That's bad

intel, man. Fire the suit, and court martial the radioman. Don't tell me what I'm shootin' at. Just tell me how bright you want it to light up the sky. Get me? Tell ya the problem is—problem is we're dealin' with a freakin' enemy won't think twice about putting a machine—gun on the roof of a damn hospital! . . .

(Beat. Realizing he's gone too far.)

Anyhow, nobody said it was a easy job. Nobody lied to me, OK. I got everything I signed up for. And those Arab guys out there in their Toyota pick-ups—in them caves—out there—you saw the video where the farmers out there in the field buyin' a RPG and the Apache lights him up from like two thousand meters? Yeah. That's pretty much the routine right there. And those guys—they're getting what they signed up for. You know what I mean? And moves like that, very pro. That takes some skill. And me? I love doin' it. So don't feel sorry for me. War is bad, but war is here. I'm just happy to be in business. And like I said, I'm good at my job. All this aside, you know if we weren't in Iraq—if we weren't in Afghanistan—yer sure as shit we'd be somewhere. Supply and demand. There's never gonna be a shortage of people wanna kill a soldier . . . But, hell, I mean don't let me lie to ya. I love seein' those yellow ribbons in traffic.

KIN

Bathsheba Doran

Dramatic
Simon, forties

Simon, a college professor, tells Anna, a grad student, why he has decided to break off their affair.

SIMON: I thought it was best not to leave you dangling, you know? But at this stage of life . . . I mean . . . I know what I'm looking for, you know what you're looking for, we know what we're looking for, or maybe we don't, maybe that's the thing, maybe I don't know what I'm looking for but I know it's not you. That sounds terrible, doesn't it? But no, fuck it, I'm trying to be truthful here, let's have truth in human relations for once, how about that? Let's be truthful with one another. I mean did you think this was going anywhere? Really? Thank you. Thank you. Now I feel less like an ass. And I mean—I'm so much older than you, that's probably why you picked me, right? A father figure? You lost your dad when you were very young, right? So that was probably part of the attraction, don't you think? But that's not healthy, that's not sustainable, or maybe it is, I don't know. The point is—and this is where I'm the real asshole—I don't know what I want. Not really. I mean, sometimes I think I want something long term, but I've been married, you know? And it was no fun. Now maybe that was her, maybe that was me, maybe it was the combination but . . . but . . . I just want someone I can talk to, you know? And fuck. And we had that. I'm not denying it. We had that. But now . . . it's over, isn't it? I mean the conversation is over. Can't you just feel it? There's something dead here. The light's gone out. And if the light's gone out then put out the light. Or maybe not. I don't know . . . we could try to ignite it. But love shouldn't be so much effort. Or maybe it should. It's such a fucking construct, you know? Literature is such a fucking trap. Unrealistic expectations. I don't know. I'm just so fucking lonely. And I know you are too, maybe that's what brought us together, right? Loneliness. A love of Keats. Your mind, you have a fucking brilliant mind, you know that? Your thesis is fucking brilliant. You're going to have an incredible career, and you'll forget all about me! I'll just be some old professor of yours that you inveigled into bed with your skinny arms and your brilliant mind. Because let's be real. We admire each other but . . . this is even a little sordid. The rest of the faculty knows, I think. Clancy made a veiled comment . . . and it's not against the rules, exactly, you are an adjunct and this is the English department, we are all poets here, and poets fuck, but Clancy's comment . . . I think fundamentally . . . it made me feel cheap. And it made you . . . cheap by association . . . So I think . . . . You haven't said anything . . . . Are you going to make this hard on me? Don't. Please don't. This is just human relationships. I wrote a poem once. When I was in my thirties and I still wrote poetry. And I compared a woman's vagina to a revolving door. People come in. They go out. That's life. And you know what my simile for the penis was? A staple gun. In an office. Punch, punch, punch. Revolve, revolve, revolve. That is life. That is the fucking monotony of searching for your soul mate. Okay? I still stand by that. So just . . . Did we even love each other?

Information on this playwright may be found at www.smithandkraus.com. Click on the AUTHORS tab

Looking Again

Charles Evered

Comic
Bill, twenties to thirties

Bill is in a bar with a male friend, giving him tips about how to pick up women.

BILL: She wears a blouse like that because she wants to be able to see the extent to which you are able to keep yourself from lookin' at 'em. The point remains that the more you look at 'em, the less likely it'll be that you'll enjoy 'em someday. Be the cowboy, Steve. The cowboy doesn't look at 'em. The cowboy doesn't have to. You're supposed to be the cowboy. Used to be we'd cut down a tree and split it, throw some logs on the campfire and stir up some grub. Now what are we? We are exactly what the eunuchs who run television shows depicted us into being. Marginalized metro-sexual tubs of butter incapable of threatening our own shadows. We are confused, confounded, passive and compromised little toady boys. What are we? Are we men? Do men even really need to exist anymore? If they don't need our penises anymore to have a baby, if you don't even need to differentiate one gender from the other anymore, then why have two separate genders at all? Why don't we all just be one gender? Why don't we all just be a bunch of "Sam's" or "Terri's"—lets all cut our hair down just to the middle of our necks. Lets all wear pants or "chinos" or whatever the hell so called men wear now. Why have pants at all, when you think of it, lets just have "leg coverings" so as not to offend those who don't feel comfortable wearing pants, and better yet, lets not wear clothes at all, as wearing them is in its own way discriminatory toward those who prefer not to so publicly declare their own gender. You want to be alive again brother? You want to break the chains? Don't look at 'em.

Looking Again

Charles Evered

Comic
Bill, twenties to thirties

> *Bill is in a bar with a male friend, giving him tips about how to pick up women, and about what you have to do these days to "be a man."*

BILL: Steve, I don't want you to be offended by what I'm about to say to you because you have to understand it isn't personal, and so I don't mean any offense to you directly. But I do want to say this: You are what this society calls "a man," but in millennia before us, lets be honest—you would be a liability. I want you to imagine what good you do—really take a long hard look at yourself. I'm not talking about feeling here, Steve, I'm talking about thinking. The world is falling apart because grown men don't know the difference anymore. People think because they feel something, it must be right. No doubt Steve, you "feel" you are a good man. That you have some worth and that perhaps, someday, you will meet a woman of average attractiveness and perhaps above average breast size and you'll couple with her and the two of you will roll around in an agreed upon orgy of self delusion that allows you both to believe you matter in the world. You'll mutually agree to subscribe to some made up tenant of belief and every Sunday you will go to church and act like something means something, well it doesn't Steve. It has no meaning. And neither do you. I want you to really think about what I'm about to propose to you—and I want you to think about it like a man would. I want you to think about taking your own life, because when all is said and done, it's the only real control we can exert upon a universe that otherwise has us reeling in anarchy and randomness. Seriously think about it, Steve. And don't make a big production of it either. If you're going to take your own life, do it in a way that would seem questionable as to whether you actually did it at all. Do it with built in plausible deniability so that your mother can tell her friends it was an "accident," or some kind of mishap but for all that is right and true and good in this putrid world, Steve, do it.

THE MOTHERF**ER WITH THE HAT

Stephen Adly Guirgis

Seriocomic
Bobby, thirties

> *Bobby, an ex-con, lives with his girlfriend Veronica. He has been trying to get his life back together, but the applecart is upset when he finds a man's hat in their room. He thinks it belongs to a guy who lives downstairs. Here, he tells his cousin Julio about how he got even with the guy.*

JACKIE: Anyway, Veronica, I think, was upset about the AA woman even though for all she knows nothing happened, and so, my belief is she started fuckin' the Motherfucker With The Hat so she could prove to herself that she don't love me, but, of course, we all know she do love me, but now, I found out about it 'cuz the Motherfucker left his Hat on my table—so—I got upset, I got a gun from Chuchi, and I took the hat and the gun to the Motherfucker with the Hat's apartment downstairs, and . . . that's when a incident happened. All I did: I knocked on the door. Motherfucker with the Hat answered. I didn't say nothing. I just took the Hat—the hat from my house, tossed it on his carpet, stared him straight in his eye, cocked the gun, and shot the fuckin' Hat on the carpet. Dass all I did.I shot his Hat. Dass all. And—BELIEVE ME—the motherfucker KNEW what that was about! The problem is, the bullet went through his hat, ricko-shayed off his floor, blew out his big screen TV, and put a hole into the guy next door's apartment who was home at the time, so, I had to, like, flee . . . And now I gotta return the gun to fuckin' Chuchi, but he ain't around, so could you please hide the fuckin' gun until, like, Chuchi could be located, please?

Information on this playwright may be found at
www.smithandkraus.com. Click on the AUTHORS tab

THE MOTHERF**ER WITH THE HAT
Stephen Adly Guirgis

Seriocomic
Cousin Julio, thirties

*Jackie, an ex-con, has recently learned that his AA sponsor
has been screwing his girlfriend. He has asked his cousin to
help him confront the guy. Julio agrees to help, but he wants
to let Jackie know exactly what he thinks of him first.*

COUSIN JULIO: The reason I said I'm doing this more for your
mother's memory than for you is because, maybe I never said
this before, but, I don't like you very much. And the reason I
don't like you very much is because you think you're a nice
guy, but really Jackie, you're not that nice. You've basically
made fun of me my whole life, you talk a lot of shit, you fuck
people over—not all the time but sometimes—and really, the
space between who you think you are and who you actually
are is a pretty embarrassingly wide gap. I hope this AA thing
works out for you. Because the cousin I loved and hung out
with and played Booties Up with when I was 8—he bears no
resemblance to the little cabroncito I'm looking at right now.
When I first came to the States from PR, you had my back,
and, really, you were a hero to me. And now, Dios perdona,
the hero is a zero, mijo! My Marisol was right about you:
It's always all about Jackie. We've been married three years
now, and whenever you come by our home, you don't even
bring so much as a bag of pistachios. And yet, you see nothing
wrong with jeopardizing my relationship and my apartment
and our safety by bringing criminal things like this caca into
our home. You're not a good friend, and you're not a good
relative. My Marisol called it: You're a user. But thass okay.
And that's all I got to say on that, so you can get out of my
apartment now, and go do all those very more important
things then spending time with your cousin Julio, okay?

*Information on this playwright may be found at
www.smithandkraus.com. Click on the AUTHORS tab*

THE MOTHERF**ER WITH THE HAT

Stephen Adly Guirgis

Dramatic
Ralph D., forty-six

> *Ralph D is laying into Veronica, the girlfriend of a man whom
> he sponsors in AA, with whom he has been having sex.*

RALPH D.: Your bravado, Veronica—it's a lotta transparently
ignorant, defensive nonsense and you know it. It feels so
good when you're spewing it, right? Because it's so "how
we do"?, "in your face"?, "talk to the hand", fuckin' "you
go girl!", and all that school yard, jailhouse, hood rat bunch
a bullshit? But what happens when the rush of acting like
a fuckin animal passes, Veronica—and you've vented all
your shit, and there's nothing and no one left to lash out at,
and no more drugs till morning, and you're just all alone, by
yourself—with nothing to feel except how fucked up your
life is and how you basically just wanna die? . . . *Again?!*
Yeah, that's right. And the one person you know with the
actual means to help you, who actually got a real feeling
in his heart for you, who thinks being with you would
be nothing like "settling;" the one guy who's been there
for you for the last 2 years 24/7 whatever you need, who
jeopardized his *marriage* for you, who picked you up out
of bars when you were stumbling like a fuckin' suicidal,
homeless zombie, who took you home and *didn't* fuck you?
That guy?! Me?! Well you just went "Buck" on him, so
forget about that guy.

*Information on this playwright may be found at
www.smithandkraus.com. Click on the AUTHORS tab*

THE MOUNTAINTOP

Katori Hall

Dramatic
King, thirty-nine

> *The Mountaintop takes place in Dr. Martin Luther King's*
> *motel room in Memphis on the night before his assassination.*
> *Dr. King has just learned that he is going to die tomorrow,*
> *from someone who has God's direct telephone number. Here,*
> *he is on the phone with God trying to get Her to change Her*
> *plans.*

KING: Uhm. God? It's uhmmm . . .
(putting on his "King" voice)
Dr. Martin Luther King, J—oh, yes. Michael, to you . . . yes
ma'am . . . yes ma'am . . . yes . . . . Ma'am. God, ma'am,
you don't sound like I thought you'd sound. No, no, no.
Pardon me, if that offends. I like how you sound. Kinda like
my grandmama. Well . . . it is a compliment. I loved her
dearly . . . . I love you more, though. Camae told me that you
might be busy tonight. Oh, you have time for me? For one
of your favorites? God, are you alright? You sound hoarse.
Oh, you tired? Well, it must be tiring to be everywhere all
at the same time.
(he laughs nervously)
Well, God . . . I don't mean to trouble you, ma'am, but I
wanted to ask you something . . . You see I have always
listened to you, honored your word, lived by your word.
(he lowers his voice)
For the most part.
(Raises it back to normal.)
God, please don't strike me down for askin' this, but . . .
I want to live. I have plans. Lots of plans in my head and
in my heart and my people need me. They need me. And I
need to see them to the Promised Land.
(Beat.)
I know that's not what I said earlier tonight, I know, but . . . I

wasn't lying exactly. I just didn't know she was comin' so, so soon. I meant every word I said tonight when I spoke to those people. Dead honest! No, no, no pun intended . . . . God, I just . . . I want to see my people there, the tide is turning . . . war is becoming the order of the day and I must, I must convince them to stay vigilant . . . .We've come too far to turn back now . . . .God, listen to me . . . Who else is betta fit for this job? I mean, who will take my place?
(he hears her answer)
JESSE!?!?
(pause)
I . . . I just thought Ralph would make a better—No, no, no, no, I have not turned vain. On the contrary. I'm but a servant for you, God, ma'am. Yes, I've been a servant for you all my life. At one point in time, I might nota been up for the challenge but I knew this was all par for the course and I did your will. I honored YOUR WILL, God, ma'am. Let me not die a man who doesn't get to hug his children one last time. Let me not die a man who never gets to make love to his wife one last time. Let me not be a man who dies afraid and alone.
(long pause)
Then why'd you pick me, huh? Hmmmm, no disrespect, but if you didn't know what I could do, what my talents were then . . . . You got some nerve. Dragging me here to this moldy motel room in Memphis. To die. HUH! Of all places! Well, I am angry. There have been many a' nights when I have held my tongue when it came to You. But not tonight, NOT TONIGHT. I have continuously put my life on the line, gave it all up. Gave it all up for You and Your word. You told me, that'd I'd be safe. Safe in your arms. You protected me all this time, all this time! Glued a pair of wings to my back, but now that've I've flown too close to the sun I'm falling into the ocean of death. God how dare you take me now. NOW! I beg of you. I plead—God? Ma'am? God?

MURPH

Catherine M. O'Neill

Dramatic
Seth, forties

> *Seth, an ex-navy seal, now a sought after national political consultant on another sort of mission, instructs his newest client's naive political staff, Katie and Gary, in the realities of political campaigns. Here he tells them politics is a business and the ideals and beliefs they hold are meaningless.*

SETH: *(chuckling)* A debate? Debates? You think Joe six pack sits down in front of his television with a notebook and scores a debate? Issues are meaningless. This is a numbers game. We're selling a product. Trust me—It's not about him—

(points to Murph)

And it's not about Andrasko. It's about the strategy we put in place. Andrasko recognizes his liabilities, not too many politicians have the stomach for that. And that is what makes him dangerous. He knows what he doesn't know. And although that may seem right now like a considerable advantage to you, the Whiz will turn Andrasko's greatest liability into his greatest asset. Suddenly the fact this guy doesn't know how to run a one car funeral will be refreshing. And Whiz and his crew will be laughing all the way to the bank. Save the flag waving for the rally. This is a hostile takeover attempt of a four billion dollar a year business, with a built in revenue stream from six hundred thousand taxpayers on a bad day. And your job is to protect the product.

*Information on this playwright may be found at
www.smithandkraus.com. Click on the AUTHORS tab*

Murph

Catherine M. O'Neill

Dramatic
Seth, forties

> *Seth, an ex-navy seal, is now a sought after national political consultant. Here he attempts to explain a truth to Katie and Gary about their boss, Murph.*

SETH: Boys and girls grow up dreaming. We say you can have that dream, as long as you aren't homosexual? We don't come right out and tell them that. No, we do the ludicrous dance of equality, making sure we leave them enough subtle hints. And when they realize, they might be the thing we are hinting about, when they realize? They create a lie to save their dream. Where's the sin? You don't dream a dream unless you have the talent to go with it. Are you prohibited from your dreams because of with whom you sleep? And when we find out the dreamers had the audacity to create a story line so their dream could live; so they could actualize it—we kick them to the curb like yesterday's rubbish. Did he lie to you? Yes. Was their a better way? For this dreamer? I don't think so, not yet, not today, maybe one day, but it's not today. And when that day comes it will come from the people in the Democratic party. And that is the only reason I work in this cesspool of politics, because once and a while we have the capacity to make people's lives better, it might not be pretty how we get there, but we get there, eventually.
(beat)
We are all entitled to dreams, the least of us and the best of us.

Information on this playwright may be found at www.smithandkraus.com. Click on the AUTHORS tab

THE NAVIGATOR

Eddie Antar

Dramatic
Dave, thirties to forties

> *Dave is talking with his stockbroker, who wants to know why all of a sudden Dave is unerring in his investment decisions. What Dave can't tell him is that he has been receiving instructions from his GPS while driving around in his car.*

DAVE: Every second . . . every moment in our lives . . . every waking, breathing, Goddamn moment is filled with coin toss decisions that carry a certain amount of consequence. Most of those consequences are insignificant. Every once in a while . . . every once in a while, a decision is life and death. I'm not talking figuratively. I'm talking . . . I'm talking about actual balance of pulse and breath depending on your ability to choose right. And instead you make a left.
(emotional)
'Cause you were sure. But you were wrong. And this . . . this changes your whole outlook on life. You become terrified of making decisions, any decisions, even the smallest, because they all remind you of the one you got wrong. You understand? Then . . . all of a sudden. All of a sudden by some miracle you come upon a way, a means that lets you always choose right. You understand what I'm saying? You come upon a way so that you never have to panic, or even question the direction your taking. I mean . . . fuck . . . what do you expect me to do? Give that up?

The Navigator

Eddie Antar

Seriocomic
Dave, thirties to forties

> *Dave's GPS in his car has been directing his life; giving him
> stock and sports betting tips. Dave has been making a fortune;
> but here he tells his friend Al why he has asked him to help
> push his car off a cliff.*

DAVE: I had no control. No life. Little by little, every joy would
st—If you knew that the Yankees were going to win every
game they ever played. Every game, season, playoff, World
Series . . . Would you be happy? Hell yeah. Would you stop
watching? Hell yes. Say you were a player on that team,
you know? You're at the plate. Pitcher checks the sign,
sets . . . you hear "fastball, outside corner" or "Slider, low
and inside" or "sixty five mile an hour change-up hanging over the left part of the plate." You knew every pitch
that's coming AND it, this voice, was always, ALWAYS
right. Think about it. Would you jump on the final out of
the World Series? Would you even wear your ring? These
joys we have . . . think of every joy in life. Think of why
joy is so precious. All it's worth, it's value . . . it has value
. . . is value because of the possibility of its opposite. Take
that away and what you have left is . . . well, I don't know
what to call it . . . lifeless. I don't know about you Al, but
I'm not ready to give life up. Life gives your surprises,
surprises give you life.

Paraffin (from The Hallway Trilogy)

Adam Rapp

Dramatic
Lucas, twenties

> *Lucas, a disabled Afghanistan war vet, tells Margo, his neighbor, that he loves her. Problem is, she's married to someone else.*

LUCAS: Margo, I've been in love with you from the first moment I saw you. You and Denny had just driven home from Kenyon. It was Christmas break your junior year. You guys came into the kitchen through the garage. You were wearing a blue ski parka and your hair was really short and your face was puffy. You had a little line down your cheek from sleeping on the seatbelt. I had just been in the living room helping my mom with the tree and I saw you and it was like everything else faded away. I'm not lying, Margo. Everything faded. The walls. The kitchen table. The linoleum floor. It was like I had been visited by someone from a dream. Just you in your blue ski parka. Floating there. You spent five days in Cleveland and all I cared about was trying to find ways to justify being in the same room as you. To get close enough to smell your hair. Which actually happened once after dinner when you were clearing the table. I was rinsing plates for the dishwasher and you brushed past me and I finally smelled it. It smelled like apples. You brushed past me and I smelled apples and I grew a third lung. I was a fucking zitty-faced junior in high school and I had fallen head-over-heels in love at-first-sight with the woman who would wind up marrying my only brother. How doomed is that. Your wedding was probably the worst day of my life. I don't even want to tell you what was going through my head as you were coming down the aisle. I was a groomsman and I thought my heart was going to turn into a peach pit and fall out of my tuxedo sleeve. I think I spent the next year trying to kill that vision of you in that dress. Every time I closed my eyes I would see you. Margo, every morning when I wake up all I can think about is you. How you're doing, if your back hurts, if your feet are swollen, what music you might be listening to, what you're wearing, what you're not wearing . . . Why do you think I wanted to spend the summer here? It was perfect—I'd be across the hall! I mean it doesn't even make any sense—I'm stuck in a wheelchair on the third floor of a fucking walk-up. I spend more time looking out the window than an international spy. I've left the building once this entire summer. July Fourth Weekend. I humped down the stairs on my hands and Marty wheeled me over to Sixth Avenue and I ate a slice at Ray's Pizza and then we went and watched a basketball game at the West Fourth Street courts. And the whole time I wanted to be back here because you and Dena had gone to see Denny's band play and I knew you'd be coming home. Sometimes I just sit on the other side of Marty's door and wait to hear the sound of someone coming up the stairs, hoping it's you. It's the main reason I've grown to hate everyone in this building: because they're never you when they come up the stairs. This floor is like a fucking prison, but I don't care because I get to be near you.

*Information on this playwright may be found at
www.smithandkraus.com. Click on the AUTHORS tab*

PASTIME

Greg Owens

Comic
Casey may be a performer of any age

Casey relates, to the audience, his story of the 'big game' during which, after being hit (intentionally, he believes) by a pitch, he smashes in the skulls of all nine of the opposing players.

CASEY: He's standing there on the mound. Grinning at me. Making fun of me with his eyes. I shoot him a grin right back: "You don't scare me you little shit." He goes into his wind-up and hurls one right at me. Catches me square in the chin. I rush out to the mound, swingin' my bat at him. He puts his hands up, tryin' to protect himself. And I let him have it. WHAM! Right on the head.
(CASEY pantomimes smashing the players' heads with his bat as he names them.)
The catcher runs up. WHAM! The infield rushes the mound. And I let 'em have it. WHAM! Second baseman. WHAM! Third base. WHAM! Shortstop. WHAM! First baseman. The outfield! WHAM! WHAM! WHAM!
(beat)
I dropped 'em all.
(pause)
I look down and my old Louisville Slugger's covered with blood. It's running down onto my hands. I look down at the field and it's soaked with blood and brains. All kinds of brain junk leaking out of their skulls. I'm standin' in it, ankle deep.
(beat)
And the fans are goin' nuts. They're laughin' and clappin' and cheerin'. "Hooray! Hooray!" I look down at all of 'em. I spit a wad of chew right in the pitcher's eye. Nobody brushes back the Mighty Casey.

Information on this playwright may be found at www.smithandkraus.com. Click on the AUTHORS tab

The Release of a Live Performance

Sherry Kramer

Seriocomic
Scott, late twenties-early thirties

> *Scott is an asshole. At least he is, tonight. He thinks he's
> General Sherman, cutting a swatch across America, trying
> to drink every drop and sleep with every woman on his own
> bachelor pilgrimage to the altar. He's wearing a cowboy hat
> and boots but he's no cowboy. He's an investment banker
> from Houston. The trucker who gave him a ride, Brent, has
> just run for the bathroom after eating a 72 ounce steak in an
> hour, leaving Scott in a strange living room with a woman
> he doesn't recognize. But fate has brought him back to the
> town he grew up in, and the woman, Coco, is the little girl
> who fell in love with him 20 years ago.*

SCOTT: *(Enters stumbling drunk into a living room he's never
been before. Sees Coco, a very nice looking woman his age,
alone there.)* Hey, did he make it? Brent, did you make it?
See, Brent, I tole you you'd make it. Tole the ole boy he'd
make it. And I'm gonna make it.
(singing)
"I'm getting married in the morning
Ding, dong, the bells are gonna chimmmmmeee—"
(Scott sees Coco. He goes over to her.)
You ever notice the Freudian implications of that song?
They're there all right. You start off—he's getting married
in the morning. Now what, you say, what is so fuckin' ac-
cordion Freudian about that? Well, I'll tell you. It's like
this. It's like from the beginning of recorded time. You
know the story of Abraham and Isaac? Everybody knows
the story of Abraham and Isaac. Everybody knows God
said "Take him out and cut him open. Sacrifice him. To
me." Everybody knows how it turned out. What they don't
know, is that God specifically specified for it to happen in
the morning. God said "Abe, babe, you gotta slip out early

in the morning, before Sarah wakes up and sees you on the lam." On the lamb—
(Scott "Baaas" like a lamb)
—get it? "Sneak out before the bitch throws a monkey wrench" is what he probably said. Cause God was wise to the ways of women. Think he would have gotten a tumble if he'd asked Sarah to go out and take a kitchen knife to the joy of her old age? No Way. And so it has been, even unto this day. A man wants to go hunting, fishing, a man wants to do any of the things a man wants to do a woman doesn't want him to, he sneaks out to do it in the morning. I don't mind telling you, I insisted on a morning wedding. But it doesn't stop there. No sir. "I'm getting married in the morning Ding dong de dumdum dumdum da aaaa" Dong, get it? Oh yeah, ding dong the bells are gonna chime. That's what happens, all right. Ring 'em and they chime. Cause ole Brent's gonna get me to the church on time.
(He bends down and looks at Coco closely.)
You look familiar. But that don't mean anything. You all look alike.
(He takes off his cowboy hat with his left hand, a sweeping gesture.)
Allow me to introduce myself. I'm a buddy of ole Brent's— picked me up outside of Houston. See, I'm hitching my way to get hitched. I'm getting married in the morning, see, so I'm hitching my way to get—aw, forget it.

Information on this playwright may be found at www.smithandkraus.com. Click on the AUTHORS tab

ROGER AND VANESSA

Brett C. Leonard

Dramatic
Roger, forties

Roger tells Vanessa of his desire to be a singer.

ROGER: *(explodes)* I been bustin' my mothafuckin' ass learnin' this shit, studyin' an' practicin' an' all that shit, an' now ya decide ta talk this I can't fuckin' sing bullshit?! Now ya gonna go an' do this? "We gonna be a team baby. We gonna play nightclubs. We gonna cut a record an' get outta here someday. We gonna be mothafuckin' famous." 'Cide ta hit me wit' all this bullshit—I'm barefoot, issat it?! I'm the one who's got no fuckin' shoes?! Where's the kitchen?! Where's the GODDAMN kitchen?! Well, fuck you! YOUR mother's the whore! So fuck you too!! And besides, I think I can sing. I know I ain't good as you, but that shit don' mean I ain't no good at all. An' you ain't no Mario-fuckin'-Lanza your ownself, if what we're doin' here all a' sudden is bein' honest with each other. If what we're doin' here is shootin' straight, issat it? Even 'bout shit can hurtchyour goddamn feelings? I don' look no good no more, don' know how ta fuckin' sing—what else ya wanna tell me ya ain't never toal my shit before? C'mon, what else?

Information on this playwright may be found at www.smithandkraus.com. Click on the AUTHORS tab

Rose (from The Hallway Trilogy)

Adam Rapp

Seriocomic
Lucas, twenties

> *Jerry, a slightly addled young man, is in love with a woman who lives in his apartment building. Here, he asks her sister Megan, who also lives in his building, if she has a clue as to why the woman he's crazy about won't give him the time of day.*

JERRY: Why won't she marry me?! She won't even give me a chance! Is it because I'm not interested in playing Bridge in East Hampton or spending weekends on the Jersey shore with all of those rich fools?! Those withering lobsters parading around in their Coupe de Villes and Eldorados?! I'm an educated man, Megan. I went to Princeton University! I could have gone to medical school! I graduated magna cum laude! I choose to work in the subway tunnels—I choose to do that! To work among the common people is important to me! To work! That doesn't mean I don't have something to offer a woman! That doesn't mean a man doesn't have character or so much love in his heart it could burst! Your sister didn't even go to college! In fact, she can't even get a job as a secretary! You know how I know? Because I followed her to an interview at Sullivan and Cromwell last week. I walked all the way down to Broad Street. I watched her stop and feed the pigeons on the corner of Canal and Church. And I saw her buy a pretzel off of a wagon two blocks later! And she went back to him for mustard and a napkin! And I saw her check her reflection in the window of a parked cab on Duane Street. I watched her all the way to Broad Street. I spied on your sister! I saved her life, Megan. I love her so much, Megan. From the moment she stumbled on the subway platform . . . I grabbed her around the waist . . . The express train rushing by . . . She gave herself to me . . . Right there in my arms, she surrendered. It was the smallest thing but I've never known anything more definite.

> *Information on this playwright may be found at*
> *www.smithandkraus.com. Click on the AUTHORS tab*

Rose (from The Hallway Trilogy)

Adam Rapp

Seriocomic
Richard, twenties to thirties

Richard has come to the apartment building where this play takes place to look for his wife Rose, who has disappeared. He has reason to believe she may have come here. He is talking to a denizen of the building, asking if anyone has seen her.

RICHARD: Hello. Dick Bumper, Metropolitan Life Insurance. You live in the building? You live here with your family? . . . You look like the family type. You gotta wife, I'll bet. Little boy, little girl. You know, they just found out that smoking cigarettes causes lung cancer. I just quit myself. Lucky's. LSMFT. Lucky Strike Makes Fine Tobacco . . . You employed? I didn't catch your name . . . what's your name? . . . Heck, it doesn't matter anyway, what matters is that you're family's taken care of. Especially these days. These are uncertain times. And what a man needs for him and his family is security. With the death of Stalin and the Russians building all those missiles, who knows what's gonna happen to our future. If one of those babies hits, we Americans may be faced with some serious problems. And that's why there's no better time to purchase an insurance policy from Metropolitan Life. If something were to happen to you . . . say you're walking out the door to go buy a newspaper . . . and zap, you're vaporized by an A-bomb . . . what's your family gonna do? They'll be up shit's creek without a paddle . . . excuse my French but allow me to continue. That brochure there breaks it all down for you. The premium payment for our new policies is quite low. Check those numbers out. Those numbers do not lie, friend—You're eating it . . . I'll bet it's delicious. I don't blame you. What a bunch of crap, right? You try knocking on doors and doing that seven days a week, ten sometimes twelve hours a day. After a while the sound of your own voice just becomes repulsive. Like some awful clarinet hitting all the wrong notes. The truth is I'm looking for my wife. Her name is Roselyn. Roselyn Bumper. Sometimes she tells people her name is Rose because, well, because she thinks it's her stage name . . . Rose Hathaway. I have a sneaking suspicion that she tried to come here today. Well, it's more than a sneaking suspicion, because I actually read about it in her journal. Probably not the most trustworthy thing a husband can do, but I felt I had the right and I'll explain. You see, my wife is an actress and last year she came very close to landing a role in a revival of this big fancy play on Broadway, but she didn't get it and she got very blue, really down in the dumps. She wouldn't get out of bed sometimes. And if she would she would just stare off into space. In the middle of the night she walked into our neighbor's house and started to . . . well, let's just say some very embarrassing things happened. Things got so bad that I took her to be psychologically examined. She took all sorts of tests. This one doctor from the National Institute of Mental Health even suggested that she try floating in a sensory deprivation chamber. She would have to float for hours on end in a large vat of saltwater. Like some awful paralyzed sea creature. The bottom line is she really hasn't been well and I thought I could help in some small way. So what I did was I forged a letter from the playwright. He was at the audition you see. According to my wife he even shook her hand. The letter I wrote to her was very flattering and it really made her feel better. It really did make a world of difference for a while. And last night he died and I read in her journal that she believed he was still alive . . . that he'd set the whole thing up and faked his own death. So she decided that she would come find him here. To thank him I guess, I don't know. And the reason she came here is because I looked in the phone book and found a Eugene O'Neill living at this very address. He's the playwright, you see, the one who she thought wrote her the letter. Well, to make a long story short, she disappeared today. We live in Connecticut . . . in Darien . . . and when I came back from my door-to-doors this afternoon she was gone. I normally wouldn't work on a Saturday, but things have been really stiff lately. Really hard-up. They've been . . . Well. Let's just say they've been hard. We're expecting our first child. We just found out a few weeks ago, so . . .

(From his briefcase RICHARD produces a copy of Rose's headshot.)

That's her there. She's beautiful, right? I wanted to give her something. She was so heartbroken. They said she was suffering from depressive tendencies . . . acute melancholia, I guess they call it . . . and they gave her a round of electroshock treatments, which is not an easy thing for anyone to go through. She barely remembered how to tie her shoes for a while. They suggested I have her committed, but I refused because I don't think she's crazy. She's just confused . . . Do you speak English?

Information on this playwright may be found at www.smithandkraus.com. Click on the AUTHORS tab

Row After Row

Jessica Dickey

Dramatic
Tom, mid-late thirties or early forties

> *Tom is a veteran Civil War re-enactor and has just finished
> re-enacting his favorite battle of the Civil War, Pickett's
> Charge at Gettysburg. He is currently torn between strik-
> ing for better wages as a local teacher, or signing the new
> contract and protecting his salary for his new family. He
> is talking to a pair of other re-enactors.*

TOM: The most amazing thing to me is that the rebel army knew
it was going to be bad and they charged anyway. You know
what I mean? And at every moment, every step along the
way, they could've turned back, like fuck this. I mean picture it—here's the start point for the Confederates, right?
*(Her gets up and illustrates Pickett's Charge—sets the
space.)*
And like, here's where the Union army is well entrenched,
right?—So the rebels walk into this open field, a mile of
marching ahead of them—long range artillery firing away,
thousands of men waiting on the ridge to kill them—and
they make it all the way across Emmittsburg Road, canon
fire, death all around, they could've turned back—they pass
Cotori farm, around here, they could've turned back—they
get all the way to the stone wall, where it turns into a fuckin'
bloodbath—bayonets stabbing, guns firing like three feet
away, punching—And even THEN! . . . The courage of that.
What makes someone do that? I don't think I could do that.
I come play soldier at Gettysburg because let's face it, I'm
gonna go home and have dreams and get up and go teach,
and go home and have dreams and get up and go teach, and
then have a holiday because it's time to have a holiday, and
then go home and have dreams and get up and go teach.
I hate this fucking piece of paper. This piece of paper makes
me feel like a piece of shit. I'm so sick of only having $168

extra a month—for anything—a beer or a birthday—I don't need to be rich or anything, but $168? It's no fucking life. It makes me want to just kick something. Or stab it. Just kick it and stab it and—kick it—and tell it not to fucking tread on me.

RX

Kate Fodor

Seriocomic
Phil, thirties to forties

> *Phil is a research physician who works for a large drug
> company. He is working with people who have agreed to be
> part of a clinical study testing a new rug which purports to
> alleviate depression in the workplace. One of his patients,
> Meena, has told him that she once published a collection of
> prose poems. Phil has purchased a copy and is here telling
> Meena that he really liked what he read.*

PHIL: I liked the poem about the day everyone in the world was
    barefoot. I don't know a lot about prose poems, but I thought
    it was—And the little girl's feet, how they were soft and
    pink like the interior of a—I thought it was very evocative,
    the one about the feet. Actually, I had a dream after I read it.
    I was back in Chicago, in the emergency room at Hartnett
    Hospital, which is where I did my internship. And I walked
    out into the waiting area and I looked at all the people. And
    you know, there's always a guy with a blood-alcohol level
    of point-four who's using an oily rag for a tourniquet be-
    cause he tried to open a beer with his chainsaw, and there's
    always an old lady puking and praying the rosary because
    she didn't throw away the chicken that was 29 days past
    its sell-by date, and there's always a five-year-old with an
    ugly rash and a high fever whose mother waited too long
    to bring him in because she wanted to beat her best score at
    Tetrus. And I thought, you know I really thought I wanted
    to do emergency medicine when I was in school, I really
    did. But after a while, I deeply hated my patients. I mean,
    I'm not entirely sure that you deserve our help here, people.
    Because we're really tired and we have $300,000 worth of
    student loans to repay, and you know, maybe what needs to
    happen here is that you need to start taking a little respon-
    sibility for yourselves! But in this dream, I was back there

and the waiting room was really crowded, and everyone in there was barefoot. Like in your prose poem. And somehow seeing their feet, it made me feel some compassion again. It made me want to be of service to them. Do you have any other prose poems I could read?

SCOTCH AND WATER

Brett C. Leonard

Charlie, sixties

Charlie explains to Danny, 30, his life-long feelings of inadequacy. He invites him to stick around awhile . . . or hit the bricks.

CHARLIE: LISTEN CUNT! You don't know what it's like to be told you're absolutely nothing since the day you were born. What it's like to be lied to your entire life. By your mother, your teachers, your friends. Your fucked-up stepfather with the hangover breath. To have ulcers at the age of thirteen! Not thirty when you probably deserve them—but thirteen—thirteen years old—livin' on antacids—listenin' to the radio. What it's like to overcome the lies and the fears, and the pains in your gut and to move on, and search and find, love. To find a woman, a special, beautiful, god-sent-from-above-angel that teaches you, shows you, the life you used to be unable to even imagine. To join her at an altar and feel for the first time, the first time in your life, that you are not only entitled to, but that you have achieved, perfection. To raise a family with that woman. Three children that recite poetry when they speak. And dance when they walk. And glow while they're sleeping. And YOU don't know. You have no idea. How it feels to lose them because of drink. To have lingering feelings from your childhood that convince you, you do not deserve this woman. You do not belong in the same room with these angels. The insults. The tears. The beatings. Have been tattooed to your soul. They are deeper than you were ever aware. And the drink helped to relieve the weight of it. And to realize, it is you, and not the drink, or the family, that is to blame. I will change, you say. I will never stay out again. I will never raise my voice, or my hands to you again. And you come home one day with flowers in those hands to deliver your new found self to your wife and kids. And all you find is a little note. On the refrigerator. Under some sort of Disney magnet. And it reads . . . . Under a Dumbo magnet . . . and all is says is they've left you for good this time. "This time, Charlie, this time we've left you for good." And you have the nerve to waltz in here, you little cunt, spouting off about an ulcer in a thirty year old body. Sleepless nights. A high I.Q. You have interrupted my day. You have ruined it, in fact. You have intruded my existence. Now—if you want to stay here with us—in our little family here—grab a stool and have a drink. Or you can leave through that goddamned door—'cause I'm tired of listening to you bitch—and I think I need another cocktail.

Information on this playwright may be found at
www.smithandkraus.com. Click on the AUTHORS tab

Sex Curve

Merridith Allen

Comic
Josh, twenty-five to thirty

*Josh's beautiful, brainy neighbor Marissa is a biochemist who
has created a serum in order to control who a person falls in
love with. Intrigued by the idea, Josh offers to help Marissa test
out her serum in exchange for a business partnership. However,
complications arise when Marissa and Josh begin to fall for each
other and finally, Josh confesses his true feelings to Marissa.*

JOSH: I'm it! I'm the reason Marissa's success rate is so low!
You see, Professors, Marissa developed a chemical substance
meant to be used just by women. It was supposed to block
the release of the oxytocin hormone so a woman could
experience free will in terms of picking her partners. It also
works on homosexual men. At least, it did work on her and
her test subjects in the beginning. Until me. I asked Marissa
to be a part of her experiment. I was the one straight guy
involved in all of this. So she had to alter her serum to fit
my biological needs. And while she was distracted with that,
she didn't realize what was really happening. The charming
effects of her serum began to wear off on her and the rest of
her test subjects. And then everything started unraveling. So
you see, because of me, Marissa was delayed in finding the
right results and solution for her experiment. Now I'm not
a scientist, or any other kind of expert, but I happen to have
a pretty good memory. I see something, I remember it. And
based on what I saw with Marissa's project, I think she should
revisit what happened; look at every detail over and over until
she can find another way to attack the problem. Because the
serum didn't work for me either. I'm afraid I fell in love, and
nothing about this experiment could stop that.

*Information on this playwright may be found at
www.smithandkraus.com. Click on the AUTHORS tab*

SEX LIVES OF OUR PARENTS

Michael Mitnick

Comic
Elliot, twenties

Earlier, Elliot has run into his ex-girlfriend Hannah making out with a stranger in a bar. Imbued with courage (and possibly alcohol), he calls her and asserts himself.

ELLIOT: And when I saw you, with . . . with your arms around that . . . guy, I wanted to kill myself. God, Hannah, I mean, he wasn't even that attractive. I could only see the back of his head, but I've seen better backs of heads. Still, guess what, Hannah? Guess what? You make this really annoying noise when you lick yogurt off a spoon.
(He imitates the sound four or five times.)
You broke my heart . . . . Hey ya know what, Hannah . . . I hate that dumb tattoo you got on your right shoulder. 'A for Anarchy.' I know I told you it was cool, but it's actually really friggin stupid. What kind of anarchist makes custom jewelry? You went to Mt. Holyoke for Christ's sake. Your Dad pays your VISA. But what I'm calling to say is . . . Hannah . . .
(heartfelt—he realizes it himself)
Someone can like me. Someone can find me attractive. Someone can actually want to be with me. It doesn't always have to be the other way around.
(remembering why he was placing the call)
So . . . in conclusion, bend over, fuck yourself in the dick and I wish you my best. My number's the same if you want to call me back.
(Elliott ends the call and smiles.)

*Information on this playwright may be found at
www.smithandkraus.com. Click on the AUTHORS tab*

SHOTGUN

John Biguenet.

Dramatic
Beau, thirties

> *Beau Harlan, a white carpenter in his thirties who has lost his*
> *house in New Orleans in the flood following the collapse of*
> *defective federal levees throughout the city, tells his African-*
> *American landlady over a bottle of bourbon how his wife died*
> *in the aftermath of the levee failure five months earlier.*

BEAU: We stayed through the storm, me and Audrey and Gene.
It passes by, and nothing to show for it. I'm already thinking I'll be back at work the next morning, lose just the one
day's wages—until we see the water coming down the street
from both directions. Next thing we know, we're in the attic
with water up around our ankles and still getting deeper.
My daddy, he gave us an ax for a housewarming present.
Said keep it in the attic case you ever need it. Everybody
took it as a joke, but Daddy tells me before the party's over,
just put it up the attic like I said. It's not such an easy thing,
though, swinging an ax upside down against the roof in a
low attic. That's three-quarter inch plywood, roofing. The
water's everywhere and still coming. I hit the wood false,
and the ax slips out of my hands. So I reach down to pick it
up, and my arm's up to the elbow in water before I find it in
the dark up there. I tell you, I swung the ax like John Henry
after that—and finally it gives way, the plywood. I chop a
hole in the roof, and the three of us, we shimmy up out of
there. Plywood, though, it don't cut clean with an ax. The
hole's jagged as a broken window. We all get cut up pretty
good coming out onto the roof, Audrey worst of all.
(pause)
Next day, man come by in a flatboat just before noon, offers to take us to the overpass of the Interstate, we want.
Says you can't believe the way it looks, everywhere he's
been so far.

(pause) Thing is, the gutter's all torn loose somehow, and everything floated to the surface, it's trapped up there between the gutter and where we are. So the boat can't get close enough to tie up to our roof. "Swim for it," he says, the man. I mean, we only talking fifteen, maybe twenty feet tops, we got to swim—and he drags us up into the boat fast as he can once we get there. But Audrey's got this wide-open gash runs down her thigh, and she won't get in the boat till Gene goes first. She's hanging on the gunnel, waiting her turn in all that filthy water. I'm trying to shoulder the boy up over the side, and somehow Audrey's hand slips. When she comes up, she's choking, spitting out the water. *(pause)* They still don't know what was in it. The doctors told me we had two hundred thousand cars submerged. So gasoline, they said, and all those chemicals and poisons people got around the house and rivers of raw sewage floating down the street. The doctors said they didn't know what the hell they were dealing with. The next day it's got to be a hundred degrees on that overpass when they finally put us in a bus to Baton Rouge. Audrey, though, she's shivering with fever. I tell the driver take us to a hospital. But no, he says, he's got his orders. They drop us off at some basketball gymnasium and leave us there. I start looking for a doctor, but there's none that I can find. So we wait a bit, see whether the fever maybe breaks. Next morning, she's looking better. The worst is over, I think. The next few days, she's weak but not so hot. I tell her we ought to see a doctor. She says it's just the sun from a day on the roof and another on the overpass. By the weekend, I think she's got it licked. Then Sunday night the fever, it comes roaring back. They take her to the hospital. *(pause)* Audrey, she don't get better, she don't get worse. Then one night someone comes wakes me up. Says there's a police car waiting to take me and Gene to the hospital. That's all they know, but hurry up they say. *(pause)* We get there, and the infection, they can't control it anymore. It's eating her alive, they say. And nothing left they haven't tried already. I touch her, and she's burning up. *(pause)* She didn't last the night.

Information on this playwright may be found at
www.smithandkraus.com. Click on the AUTHORS tab

A SMALL FIRE

Adam Bock

Dramatic
John Bridges, fifty

John is describing his daughter Jenny's wedding party to his blind wife Emily.

JOHN: It's so strange to look out over this wedding. It looks like a high school or it's like a high school reunion. Over near the stone wall there's a crowd of Jenny's lawyer friends They look like the jocks and Bob Ramsey looks like a coach or a guidance counselor and she Miriam Lester she'd be the librarian. Her hair is tied back super tight. Tight. And there are all these pretty girls. And everyone is huddled in their groups. It's always the same story. They didn't get that cake. They just got a bunch of plates on this tiered thing with cupcakes on it. It's pretty but it's not a cake. Henry's uncle Puddy was playing drums in the band. And Henry's dog. They put a giant orange and green ribbon around its collar. Stanley Williams and Janet are sitting with Tom and Bayla. You should see how bored Bayla looks and Tom looks drunk. His ears are red. Stanley won't stop talking. He's just Alex McCready is sitting at the table next to them. He told me that his daughter is going to graduate school for architecture and he was saying she'll be building skyscrapers and maybe you could give her her first job when she gets out of school but she was laughing and she told me it's some kind of computer information architecture or something that the kids are building on the Web. I put Juan Pujadas at Alex's table and I think he's flirting with Alex's daughter. Because she keeps tilting her head down and looking up at him like Princess Di and then she She just did it again She looks up at him and then she laughs.George just stood up on his chair. That's him yelling. He's Something about the strength of a marriage being like a truck and the four wheels of a truck I dunno. Lynn just threw a dinner roll at him. And. Now. Oh. She's trying to pull him down off Oh there Oh there Oh oh oh oh oh Emily he's down she pulled him down oh he's up he's laughing he's laughing and hugging her and oh oh they're Now they're dancing.I wish you could see the little Schwartz twins Peter Schwartz's little girls they're cute and they're both dancing with him and with their mom.

(He cries. Then.)

They are. I wish you could see all of this. The light is so beautiful and the tent and the lights in the tent are so beautiful and they did everything in pink and this pinky-orangy and soft green and the light is soft and the light on the cedars that line the lane leading up to the house is beautiful and friendly and everyone looks so bright and warm and our sweet girl Jenny looks beautiful and everyone is so proud of her and smiling at her and she's smiling and it's something.

Information on this playwright may be found at www.smithandkraus.com. Click on the AUTHORS tab

A SMALL FIRE

Adam Bock

Dramatic
Billy Fountaine, 40

Billy is comforting and advising John Bridges. John is the husband of Billy's boss and friend Emily Bridges, who is struggling with a mysterious illness that is slowly depriving her of all of her senses.

BILLY: Your wife is my friend. You know, you're not the only one who's had something like this happen to him. I had a partner, Dion, he was my first partner, my first real, he was the only guy I really loved, before Richard. He was positive when I met him. He was positive but he was healthy. This was fourteen years ago. All around us. We had friends I'd visit them in hospice and sleep there, these little twin beds. And Dion was in the choir at our church and he sang at so many services. But me and Dion. He was always healthy and I'd knock wood I was so grateful—look at us—look how lucky we are, I'd think. But one day, suddenly, he got sick. It was scary. Because Why's this happening? and What's happening? and What's going to happen next? I can remember it so vividly. You don't know what to do. I remember walking down the street Wanting to scream at everyone "How are you going on with your lives, don't you know that —" Or you think "If I just hold my breath, if I'm just quiet enough, Death will walk by and He won't notice us." Then he died. On a Monday at 10:27 in the morning. We were watching Rosie O'Donnell and halfway through her show he died. Not that Rosie killed him. Your wife was so good to me. The whole time. I'd only been working for her for a couple of years and I was a mess, I was sleepwalking through work. She was so kind to me. She never said anything but sometimes she got the guys to leave me alone and sometimes she got them to make sure I wasn't alone. Sometimes she'd be "Come on Billy! Get going!" She took care of me and I promised myself, if I could ever do anything for her, I was gonna. So. You mind if I say one thing? You gotta keep doing stuff. This can be a disaster or it can be an opportunity. Somehow. You can try to shove everything back to the way it was, to try to approximate it, to almost be how you were before or you can say "Everything's different and maybe I can be different" because it's a chance to change stuff and stuff you might not have been able to change before. You gotta live a little bigger than you think you can. Somehow you gotta still see her. Because she's still here. And life is short.

Information on this playwright may be found at www.smithandkraus.com. Click on the AUTHORS tab

SUNLIGHT

Sharr White

Dramatic
Matthew, mid-sixties

> *Matthew Gibbon, liberal lion and president of a private*
> *Northeastern university, has vandalized the office belonging*
> *to the conservative dean of the law school (and Matthew's*
> *son-in-law). He is now under threat of a no confidence faculty*
> *vote and the Board of Regents is seeking to expel him. He*
> *speaks to Maryanne, his decades-faithful assistant.*

MATTHEW: I tell you. You wake up one day and realize no
one's thought to inform you it's a different world. You know
what I miss? A good old-fashioned sense of outrage, Midgie.
Where's the outrage, at the right people, not at me, not at
some . . . some . . . minor university president.—You don't
have to point it out to me, I know it's true, God knows I
wanted to do more, be more, be . . . larger. In the world. And
yet the law school, they arrive at the meeting as if I am the
mover of worlds: How dare I! Smash Vincent's office!—
allegedly—The horror! While most of them will forever
have blood on their hands from the documents they've
drafted. Out there . . . somewhere . . . hundreds of people
we've racked and tortured. And the law school are livid!
At my outrage! Upon discovering that my . . . my protege
. . . this . . . this brilliant young man . . . Why did I take
him under my wing, we disagreed on almost everything,
but it was a harmless choice at the time, wasn't it, we were
at the apex of our great Pax Americana, his brand of legal
revisionism belonged at a university! And then the planes
hit . . . It'll always be a knife in my guts, Mimi, this . . .
Pandora's Box we've opened, of barbarity. But instead of
all the ills of man springing forth it's a legion of fellows
in navy sport coats with their lecterns and legal theories,
and no matter how hard you try, you can't stuff them back
in. And now they'll always be here, ready to call out their

Armies of the Night against any who oppose them,—Well, almost any, I mean look at tonight! Turns out I've got the . . . the fucking Department of Performing Arts on my side— that's a big relief! We've got student mimes pretending to be trapped in a box with the board of regents! Whoopdeedoo! What's worse, I'm . . . I'm grateful for the support! In what . . . strange world have I awakened! Standing. And showing their backs to me.

Information on this playwright may be found at
www.smithandkraus.com. Click on the AUTHORS tab

SUNLIGHT

Sharr White

Dramatic
Vincent, mid-forties

> *Vincent Krieger is the conservative dean of the law school
> at a private Northeastern university helmed by his father-in-
> law, a liberal lion, who has vandalized Vincent's offices and
> set off a firestorm of controversy. Vincent speaks to his wife,
> Charlotte, and his father-in-law about his decision to work
> in the Bush administration's legal department.*

VINCENT: Let me give you madness, OK? Madness is waking
up one morning and holding your wife's hair back while
she goes through morning sickness, and getting her on the
early train to Manhattan and then preparing for your day,
getting to the office, prepping your first lecture, and then
your assistant turning up white in the face and ushering
you to the television where a crowd has gathered, your
assistant telling you she's already tried reaching your wife
a half dozen times and you becoming quite frantic. With
every passing minute. Where is she, is she safe, is she
alive, they say people are jumping, is she jumping, has my
wife jumped. That's madness. Three days later your wife
is bleeding and you've never really been allowed to TALK
ABOUT ANY OF IT!
(desperately holding back emotion)
And apparently trying again will always be out of the question. I don't know why I bring it up so much in my lectures,
Charlotte, I don't know why it's all I can think about some
days, but it seems like the more you pull away from me the
more I obsess over what happened. I mean I know the facts,
but the little details I admit to having totally made up, that's
madness too. But true madness? Is . . . is knowing. Knowing.
That you were there. That this was not a dream, this was not
just some day we try not to think about, that this was . . . was
. . . was real. Knowing this and yet NOT doing everything,

everything, everything to see that it doesn't happen again, including committing acts that during any other time in our history would be regarded as questionable. It's funny that you're calling me radicalized, Matt, because in this situation frankly I have to say you're the radical one, seriously, take a long drive across this country you'll meet very few people who don't believe in torture, they really don't know what the big deal is. Even me, I have the facts telling me that ultimately torture doesn't work, I should be smart enough to overcome what is probably an animal inclination towards sheer, impractical revenge, but I can't. I can't close the door on the fact that I think physically, psychologically ruining somebody should be available to us.

(silence)

We didn't know the ages, or identities, or situations, of anyone. All we had were piles of urgent requests. And at the time our reply to every fax was The President has declared the Geneva Conventions do not apply to enemy combatants. Everybody knew what that meant. And if they say they didn't, they're a liar.

Information on this playwright may be found at
www.smithandkraus.com. Click on the AUTHORS tab

THE TWO-MAN KIDNAPPING RULE

Joseph Gallo

Seriocomic
Jack, late twenties

While skimming through a box of memorabilia, Jack tells his best friend Vincent the story of how he met his ex-fiancée.

JACK: Look at this . . . It's a pack of matches from the After Hours Bar. This is from the night she gave me her phone number. She had just moved up here from Texas. She was teaching grade school down there, living with some guy, but . . . she wanted to be a model. When I met her she was sleeping on a friend's couch in Queens. She used to hang out in the city at the After Hours Bar. I met her there . . . I told her . . . I had to take her out for dinner. She said, "I really shouldn't . . . I'm seeing someone." I said, "I want to take you out for dinner." Then a few days later . . . ? I ran into her again. She told me her birthday was coming up the following week . . . she lied about her age by the way . . . so, I said, "Let me take you out for your birthday." She's like . . . , "I'm seeing someone!" But that night I kept talking to her, and talking to her, and then finally, she said . . . , "All right . . . you can take me to dinner." And that's when she gave me her phone number. I called her. I said, "Let's meet at The Coffee Shop." It was a Friday. I walked in the door, and I looked at her across the room, and I knew right then I was going to be involved with her . . . and it wasn't going to be casual, either. I didn't know who this boyfriend was . . . I didn't know his name . . . I didn't care. I felt no compassion for him whatsoever. All I knew was I had to have her in my life. So we drink . . . we eat . . . we go out to some dive bar . . . play the jukebox . . . shoot pool . . . we have a great time. Finally, she says, "Okay. We can go back to my house. But here's the ground rules. We can not touch each other. Don't touch me." I said, "Fine. I don't care what the rules are." I didn't want the night to end. We get back to her place . . . ? Within seconds we are all over each other. She says, "Usually I don't do this until the third date." The night ended Monday morning. By the end of the weekend I told her I had to marry her. She said, "I can't! I'm seeing someone!"

Information on this playwright may be found at
www.smithandkraus.com. Click on the AUTHORS tab

THE TWO-MAN KIDNAPPING RULE

Joseph Gallo

Seriocomic
Vincent, late twenties

> *Vincent tries to stop his heartbroken best friend Jack from following his ex-fiancée down to Texas.*

VINCENT: The love of your life . . . ? Jack . . . you get three great loves. First love. The one who got away. And the love of your life. She's the one who got away. If she was the love of your life then your life is over. The love of your life is still out there somewhere waiting for you. You act like I don't know what I'm talking about here. Like I haven't been burned before . . . ? I was quasi-engaged once. Stacey . . . ? You move on. You kill the love. You say good-bye once and for all. It's only hard because you're the one who got dumped. She left you and now you're stuck like Wednesday right in the middle. You can't move ahead. You can't move back. And so now you're destined to spend hours of worthless energy obsessing about what you can't have. Understand something, Jack . . . when two people get together . . . either they stay together forever or they break up. It's that simple. It's that black and white. Of course, one of them could die, which is essentially a really, really bad break up . . . Do you know what your problem is, Jack? I'll tell you. I could line up Sigmund Freud . . . Dr. Phil, Kelly Clarkson, and all of them would tell you the exact same thing . . . , "Move the fuck on." But right now it makes no difference to you. I could smack you every morning in the head with a 2 x 4 labelled - SHE'S GONE AND IT'S OVER - and still it wouldn't make a lick of difference. And do you know why . . . ? Because the heart will kick the brain's ass every time. Even if the brain's message is . . . , "You two weren't meant for each other." *(pause)* I repeat . . . , "You two weren't meant for each other." What I should have done is told you the truth the first time. Right before you got engaged, you asked me . . . , "Do you think I should get married?" And I said, "Why are you getting married?" And you said, "Well . . . I think it's time." And then we had some bullshit conversation.The truth is anyone who ever says they're getting married because "it's time" is destined for disaster. The only right answer to . . . , "Why are you getting married?" Is . . . "Because I'm in love." *(pause)* So stop acting like such a jellyfish and move on.

Information on this playwright may be found at
www.smithandkraus.com. Click on the AUTHORS tab

WAITING FOR WEINSTEIN

Robert Lundin

Dramatic
Benny, twenty-five to thirty-five

Benny is one of five mentally ill patients waiting to see their psychiatrist for 15-minute sessions. In order to kill the time, the group invents a game, "Be My Shrink," in which each one takes a turn being the patient while the other members of the group play psychiatrists, peppering the patient with questions. Here, Benny confesses to the group that he has done two years in the penitentiary, and why.

BENNY: I tried to kill my brother Sean. He don't talk to me no more. He don't have nothing to do with me. He lives with his wife in Rogers Park. I can't even go around him or his family. He has an order of protection against me. I was lookin' at ten years 'til the public defender plea-bargained it down to two years. I tried to kill him. I choked him 'til he passed out. He almost died on the way to the hospital. He doesn't want nothing to do with me anymore. He won't forgive me. I've tried. I don't know. He was my brother. I should have loved him. I love my mom and dad. I love my sister. I just hated my brother. For no good reason. We were playing a heavyweight boxing game on the computer. It was in the living room. It was in the late afternoon and he was beating me. Then I picked Hulk Hogan and he picked The Undertaker. I go out first, I was psyched. That's the best part of the game, when the wrestlers make their entrances. I started rootin' for The Hulk. My mom was out working and my dad was sleeping off a drunk. So my brother gets all mad and starts telling me to shut up because I'll wake up dad and he didn't want dad wakin' up from a drunk and coming and beating our ass. I say "Fuck you." Sean says "Fuck you" back. Then I snapped. I guess I just snapped. That's how it happened. I thought, I don't give a shit if Dad comes out here and beats both our asses. I'm gonna root for Hulk Hogan and we're gonna beat the Undertaker's ass. Then Sean turned off the Play Station. This time I really snapped. I lunged and got him by the neck. I choked as hard as I could. I was Hulk Hogan and he was every evil wrestler on the planet. He was totally evil and I was good. Sean turned blue and collapsed. I let him go. Then I snapped out of it. I realized I had killed my brother. No, not quite, he was moving and trying to breathe. I didn't want to wake up my dad so I called 911 myself. The paramedics and police got there and they did a tracheotomy and saved his life. The police arrested me and I went to jail. The posted my bail at $200,000 and no one I knew was going to come up with a $20,000 bond, so I sat in jail until my court appearance. The public defender worked out a deal that the state would drop the charge from attempted murder to felonious aggravated battery if I pleaded guilty. He said that was a good deal and I shouldn't pass up on it because any jury would convict you and I didn't stand a chance at trial. They said don't even try NGRI. That's Not Guilty by Reason of Insanity. The funny thing is, I *am* a mental case. Well, the judge was lenient and gave me two years at Joliet—could have been ten—and I did my time. But now my brother won't talk to me. I think that what bothers me most. He'll never talk to me again. He won't come home for Christmas when I'm home. At Thanksgiving, my parents tell me to get out of the house so that Sean can come home. So I hang out at record shops and sleep in my car.

Information on this playwright may be found at www.smithandkraus.com. Click on the AUTHORS tab

WHEN JANUARY FEELS LIKE SUMMER

Cori Thomas

Dramatic
Devaun, nineteen, African American

Devaun is speaking to his best friend Jeron, age 18, also African American, The two of them have decided to make signs that they will distribute, warning the neighborhood about a lecherous man they feel is dangerous to boys and men.

DEVAUN: This is good what we doin', right Jeron? I mean how we warnin' people and shit. I want to . . . I want to . . . do something you know like them posters of Malcolm and Martin or Superman? And I wanna teach people wrong from right or somethin' like that. Not like in church, 'cause that shit is borin' and it last too long, and the singin' is wack, 'cause they ain't got no good tunes. But I do like it when Reverend Buford start to clear his throat three or four times in a row, like this.
(shows him)
And start walkin' back and forth, and speakin' forcible, and his shoulders start goin' up and down like this,
(shows him)
And he start swingin' one hand with his knees bended. "yes ah." and the people in the church look like they froze up listenin'. That's what I like to see. How they can listen to that one man and he short and light skinned and plain till he open his mouth and start speaking forcible. Then it's like he a new man. Like he grew or somethin'. I study that shit, 'cause I like the idea. But it don't have to be in no church. It could be anywhere. I could just say somethin' in a corner in the street, and people will stop to listen and wave they hands 'cause in the moment they will be like feelin' the spirit of the lord or the mightiful. If I can figure out how you could get people to sit on a wood bench till they ass burn listening to me. That's when I know I will become a dude with

wimmins lining up and down the block waitin' for me. I will walk down the street, and the birds will stop flyin' and hang in the sky and look down at me like this,

(shows him)

Cats, dogs, raccoons, and wimmins and everyone. Just lookin'. At me. Like this,

(shows him)

Like, this thing we doin' to protect the people from Lorrance is helpful and important. It's a good thing, Jeron, I can feel it. Can't you? But truth is, I don't think he can really run in them shoes he wear. They got them pointed toes. Them shoes he wear look like they hurt. It's the principus of the thing. That's what it is. I'm looking for the beginning chance to show people the real meaning inside of me so they can say "Whaaat?" I just want to do something for the world to know that when we walk down the street and sidewalk, people don't think we invisible.

Information on this playwright may be found at
www.smithandkraus.com. Click on the AUTHORS tab

When January Feels Like Summer

Cori Thomas

Dramatic
Joe, forties, African American

> *Joe is speaking to Nirmala, an East Indian, woman in her
> 40's. They are in the hospital room of Nirmala's husband,
> Prasad, who is brain dead and hooked up to machines. Joe
> has developed feelings for Nirmala and come to the hospital
> to see for himself how bad the situation with her husband
> actually is.*

JOE: You and I are the ones suffering like fools thinking about
what we did to 'cause something. I was thinking about how
it seem like things I touch end up in the garbage. There's a
chain of events for things to end up in the garbage. First, it's
got to be sorted and put in the right bag. Then you put it out
on the right day in the right kind of container. If you don't
do that we won't pick it up. After you've done that, people
like me come and pick it up. Once we done the house to
house and the truck is filled, and it can hold the ten, twenty
thousand pounds or so you and your partner picked up,
once you done your regular route; you have picked up too
many bags and flattened boxes and broken things to count.
And it's a dangerous job. People don't always think about
wrapping things right. If you don't wear your gloves, if you
don't look at what you about to pick up before you actually
do, even if you do, you can get hurt. Cut by rusted metal,
burned by all kinds of putrefying substances. But I'm not
just talking about garbage you find in the street 'cause it
was thrown out. Becky, my ex, for instance . . . she seemed
fine, looked like all her parts could operate properly, we had
ourselves some nice times, and then the second night after
I had brought her home from the wedding, things began to
turn bad. Seem like I had barely just got my tuxedo off the
night before and climbed into the bed to warm it up for my
new wife. Seem like I had just finished exhaling a breath

of relief because now I was a man with a job what's got benefits and a pension and stability; a breath carrying with it the fact I was now looking forward to a future with my wife I could see myself enjoying . . . Babies and children and a house. A life. A real life. The first night was cool. But the second night while she was in the bathroom, I should have known that something was broke that no account of trying was going to fix. I could have saved myself a lot of time . . . years full of trouble. I could have stopped holding onto my dreams so tight they had to be pried from my hands still . . . still trying and trying to hold onto them . . . I should have known when she come out after staying too long in the bathroom, her eyes red, her nose running. I should have known because she seemed nervous and spoke too fast, and laughed too loud, and couldn't settle down, and then when I went into the bathroom myself and found white powder on my blue sink, I should have known and just accepted it. Seem like that experience made me feel that maybe because of my job, there's something in me that's gonna attract garbage, even though it's just the opposite of what I want, because I want jewels, I want gold and treasure, but seem like I'm scared to try again to look for it. Seem like I'm just scared now. But when I see you tending to the store, I want to pick you up . . . and handle you carefully because you're so beautiful. You're like a flower, You're like that gold earring I saw shining on the sidewalk last Thursday. Shining in the dirt, and I couldn't help but reach down and pick it up to see if it was real. I didn't know you were married, but I knew you looked too precious for my clumsy hands to reach out to try to touch.

Information on this playwright may be found at
www.smithandkraus.com. Click on the AUTHORS tab

When January Feels Like Summer

Cori Thomas

Seriocomic
Jeron, eighteen, African American

Jeron is speaking to his best friend Devaun, age 19, also African American. Jeron is very smart, but shy when it comes to talking to women—the opposite of Devaun, who is a womanizer but articulation-challenged.

JERON: I dial. She answer. I say "Hi, is this Larissa Shang?" And that's another thing, that name you gave me is wrong. Larrisa Shang don't sound like Lucy Ming, Devaun. The woman's name is Lucy. So the shit was confusing right there at the jump point. She say, "Who?" I tell her I got the number from you. She say "yeh?" I say "yeh." She say, "My name is Lucy." I say, "Oh." I want to punch you in your mouth right then. She ax me how it feel to be on TV? I say "it aiight." Then I hear some quiet silence so that I can hear her breathe over the phone. But I remember how you said to keep talkin' and put your interests up front and shit. So I ax her forcefully if she want to git wit me. She silent. I repeat it, "Do you want to git wit me?" She silent again. I repeat it a third time. "Do you want to git wit me?" That's when she say, "what do you mean?" So I say, "what do you mean, what do I mean?" She say, "What. do. you. mean?" In a real nasty tone, in a low voice sound almost like a man. So I say, "I mean git wit me. To git. wit. me. Git it? You know about that right? If your Moms and Pops ain't git together, you and all human beings might not be born." So I repeat it one more time, 'cause I don't know if maybe she don't speak English good or she slow, I say, "Do. You. Want. To. Git. Wit. Me?" That's when Lucy Ming scream "I'MA SEND SOMEONE TO FUCK YOU UP!" in my ear so loud it vibrate like a bell was ringing inside my head. But I say to myself, well, at least I know she understand me. Shit! But instead, she hang the muthafuckin phone up on me. And when I call back, she hang up soon as I said "Hello." And this right here is why I don't like to do this shit. Like callin' muthafuckin punk ass wimmin and havin' to speak to them so they can talk so loud in your ears and shit. Auno how you can think it's worth it to have so many girlfriends and what have you. Who want to git wit a woman can scream so loud anyway. I say, give me my own money, give me my own time. Wimmin is stupid. Some of em git pregnant and you gotta spend alla your lil money on Pampers. Then some of em want for you to pay for them to do they nails every week and shit. Why I want to spend my money on they nails? For what? I got more important things in the world to think about. I don't need to be talkin' on no phone to no stupid ass punk ass Lucy Ming. That's on you, telling me some lie on her. That girl ain't interested in me. And you made me call her like a damn stupid ass fool. I oughta whup you, Devaun. I oughta whup your fuckin ass.

Information on this playwright may be found at
www.smithandkraus.com. Click on the AUTHORS tab

WILD ANIMALS YOU SHOULD KNOW

Thomas Higgins

Dramatic
Jacob, teens

*Jacob is a gay kid in love with Matthew, who is straight.
Here he tells Matthew's father about how the two became
friends.*

JACOB: Some of the older boys at school, they used to, um . . .
they used to tie me to this tree. Hey that's the bargain. You
wanna do certain stuff, you wanna stay in the boy scouts?
You gotta endure other stuff too.
(beat)
But this tree, it's, um, it's actually how Matthew and I became friends again. There was kind of a massive, collective
turning on me that took place when we all started middle
school and everyone sort of dropped me. And because your
son, at the time, didn't know any better . . . he did too. Hey:
builds character, right? Can't wait to find out!
(beat)
You never noticed that I, like, suddenly wasn't around?
Anyway, it just sort of became this ritual, this . . . thing.
Like once a week or so: I'd get tied up. And it wasn't all
that bad, actually. I mean, there were a few times when
they'd put lipstick on my face, or something like that,
but—I know, right? Some asshole's bringing cosmetics to
school and I'm the fag that gets tied to a tree? But one day,
Matthew—who'd sort of always been there, but, like, in
the back of the crowd, sort of unsure at first of what to do,
you could see it, on his face—Matthew, one day, he walks
to the front of this little . . . gaggle of boys, and he says: I'll
tie him up today! Let me do it!
(beat)
And at first I'm sort of horrified, because, you know, this
feels like it will kind of complete the, um . . . the total hiatus
our friendship had taken from like 5th to 7th grade, but I

stay still, and he walks over, and then he leans into me, and he says: over the fence, around the tree, and into the rabbit hole, three times.

(beat)

And after a moment of being kind of like, um: what? I look down and he's saying it again, as he's tying me to the tree: over the fence, around the tree, and into the rabbit hole, three times.

(beat)

He'd invented this knot, see? It's a variation on a 'sheet knot' and another kind of . . . um . . . well, it's a messy looking thing, is what it is. Which is probably why the boys always wondered how I ever managed to get out. But it was this thing, this knot, that only he and I knew how to undo.

(beat)

And so every time after that, Matthew would tie the knots, and I'd know how to get out of them, and . . . and it was our thing. Which was, like, this gift. This weird kind of . . . I don't know, compassion? And . . . we became friends again.

(beat)

But I guess I'm sort of wondering, now: what kind of person comes up with stuff like that, you know? And what happens when it's, I don't know . . . used for something else?

Information on this playwright may be found at
www.smithandkraus.com. Click on the AUTHORS tab

WOOF

Y. York

Dramatic
LJ, thirty, African-American

*There was a wild and raucous party at the stadium to cel-
ebrate the start of training camp for the current Super Bowl
champions. At some point, LJ Freeman, the beloved quarterback, left the party and went to the field, where he was
caught by the security camera committing a senseless crime.
The security tapes get to the TV news and internet, and by
morning, all of America has seen them, and LJ is summarily
banned from football. He tries to explain to Mrs. Jones, his
revered, but long forgotten fifth-grade science teacher.*

LJ: I can't lift a desk, I can't even tie my shoes. I can't do anything. I don't know what to do. There's no place I can go.
I ride around with yard guys. "Where we take you, Señor
Freeman?" The only people talking to me are talking Span-
ish. It wasn't a dog jumped on my back, it wasn't a big ol'
dog, it was a Detroit Lion. Champion showed game films
at the party, he thought it would be funny—a whole reel of
me getting knocked on my ass. And there it is right in the
middle of the funny film—the end of a nothing game, we're
up three touchdowns, why am I still playing? Why am I still
throwing passes? I go back to pass, and my offensive line,
the most unbreakable line in the NFL—breaks, and a three
hundred pound Detroit Lion flattens me. Pain—fire—his
helmet in my back. The pain doesn't go away. I go to Dr
Scott cause I know he ain't gonna tell, he ain't gonna call
the newspapers. He shoots me up so I can play. But the
pain doesn't go away. I play a whole season with fire in
my back—but I throw, I always throw—It's me gets us to
the Super Bowl. The last drive of the biggest game of my
life, my arm freezes, and I call draw plays—"I'm a genius,
I fool the defense" that's what everybody says—but I'm
only handing off because my arm don't go forward! It don't

go. All spring I'm sneaking to the east side getting shot up with who knows what, but it don't go forward. And I'm supposed to start training camp—that's why they're having this party—everybody's there—all the gimme people, everybody with his hand in my pocket, helping me celebrate a new start. I'm the best quarterback in the league, except my arm don't go forward. How am I supposed to live without football? There's no money, there's nothing. The only way I have enough money is if I die.

Information on this playwright may be found at www.smithandkraus.com. Click on the AUTHORS tab

SCENES

BLOOD AND GIFTS

J.T. Rogers

Dramatic
Gromov, forties
Jim , late thirties

> *GROMOV, a KGB agent in Pakistan, is arguing with JIM, a CIA agent, about the mess in Afghanistan in the 1980s during the Soviet invasion.*

GROMOV: Since January our Fortieth Army has fought solely to defend itself against mujahideen attacks. No offensive maneuvers. Not one.

JIM: You want a medal for this?

GROMOV: Since almost one year, stated Soviet policy is we are withdrawing our forces.

JIM: Dmitri! You're promoting Najibullah to be president of Afghanistan. Your lapdog, running things in Kabul. This is your idea of "withdrawing"?

GROMOV: We don't care anymore who runs Kabul! Najibullah wants fancy new title? Fine! Let him go down in flames!

JIM: Dmitri, I'm late for a meeting.

GROMOV: No one on your side is listening. JIM: ! Get your people in Washington to open their ears!

JIM: I don't have time / for this!

GROMOV: *(exploding)* Thousands of people are dying!

(They both stop. They look around, then pull in closer.)

GROMOV: We can't get our soldiers out of Afghanistan because your Khan and the rest of your proxy fighters won't stop attacking. Because of your Stingers, our forces cannot defend themselves. All we are asking is let us withdraw without bloodbath. Leash your proxies!

JIM: They're not poodles!

GROMOV: What is this schoolyard mentality? You had your humiliation in Vietnam, so we must have ours? Jim, we are leaving with tails between legs and whole world is watching. What more do you want?

JIM: To see our obligation through. Help those men who have sacrificed their blood and lives to save their country!

GROMOV: Do you know what your "sainted angels" are doing to our soldiers when they capture now? They are skinning them alive, Jim! Tearing off flesh with knives!

JIM: And your soldiers were choir boys?

GROMOV: The Afghan people know we tried! We went there to be a force for justice! Our Union of Socialist Republics stands for the cause of liberation!

JIM: Would you get off your high horse just once! Are you going to look me in the eye and say—still!—that Moscow marched to Kabul for justice?

GROMOV: *(a moment, then quietly)* No.

(Jim stares. Not that he expected.)

GROMOV: *(slowly at first but then a dam is released)* Those senile old men hunched round Politburo table. We do not even know which of them gave order to invade. Who signed off? Who is responsible? No one knows. Suddenly, our troops were rolling and blood was flowing, and it just happened. Dinner is supposed to just happen, not war! And they knew it was lost! Five years ago they knew! Oh, but to leave without "victory," that would not be Russian! That would be "grievous blow to our world authority"! Even with your Vietnam staring us in face, still we could not learn! Because we are Russian and we learn only by suffering! Because nothing else penetrates our STUPID MONKEY SKULLS!

(Jim, as well as many other PEDESTRIANS, stares at him wide-eyed.)

GROMOV: What? Things are different now. Gorbachev says we are free to speak.

JIM: Like that? I think I prefer the old you.

GROMOV: This is what my wife says. We are on phone, she wants to speak about our Masha, but I can't stop talking about all this. Elena yells, "Stop caring about politics! Care about your daughter!"

JIM: How is Masha? Is everything . . . all right with—?

GROMOV: Yes, fine. Baby is almost due.

JIM: That's great. Congratulations.

GROMOV: Thank you.

JIM: Will she still not tell you who the baby's father is?

GROMOV: Jim! You know I have high blood pressure! Why are you bringing this up?

JIM: You're right. I'm sorry. Everything's going to work out. She's got friends, she's got her mother—

GROMOV: But her father is here. My family is there, but I am here.

GROMOV: Tell me, why did you return to be station chief again?

JIM: Usual reasons.

GROMOV: You missed the weather? Jim. You were home, with your wife. Why would you leave her, come back here?

JIM: I made a promise to see this through.

GROMOV: A "promise" is more important than your wife? Are you—what is phrase?—fucking serious? Do you know how many promises I would break to be with my wife?

JIM: I'm not done making amends, Dmitri.

GROMOV: Ahhhhh. Now you sound like Russian. Now you are finally making sense. Tehran?

JIM: Yeah.

GROMOV: Tell me.

JIM: (A moment. Then . . .) The Shah wasn't going to last. And it was not going to end well. I reported, and no one listened. I yelled, and I was told to keep my mouth shut. So I did my job. The mullahs swept in, the purges began, and I left. I left everyone who'd helped me. Assets who'd risked their lives for their country, families who'd opened their homes to me, kids I played ball in the street with. Killed. Every. Single. One.
(Neither man moves. Then . . .)

GROMOV:	JIM: When man tries to make amends, if he does not see bigger picture, matters are made worse. Tehran is only few hundred miles from Kabul. Do you think the mullahs there are not watching us?

JIM: Trust me: I will not let the Iranians come here.

GROMOV: The Iranians are only part of bigger picture, JIM: . Prisons of Egypt and Jordan, they have been cleared out. All sent here. They are not coming for vacation cruise. Every day, more and more, here to wage jihad against unbelievers. Against you and me. Jim, our republics that border this region, they are all Muslim. And these Islamists are already knocking at door. If you break our army and we do not have strength to stop them . . . When they are done with us, who do you think will be next?

AFTER

Chad Beckim

Dramatic
Monty, mid thirties, Latino or African American.
Chap, early forties, any ethnicity.

> *Following 17 years of wrongful incarceration for rape, Monty has just been exonerated by DNA evidence and released. On his second day home, his former Prison Chaplain—and friend—has arrived unexpectedly for a visit.*

> *Chap steps forward, hand extended. A half beat, then Monty shakes it.*

CHAP: I realize this visit is unexpected. I hope this isn't a problem.

MONTY: . . .

CHAP: Your sister kept me company while I waited for you. It was nice to put a face with a name.

MONTY: . . . What were you two talking about?

CHAP: *Cafe con Leche*. She gave me her recipe. *(a short beat)* Do you mind if we sit?

MONTY: . . . Go ahead.

> *(Chap sits. A half beat, then Monty sits. A long beat.)*

CHAP: So how is everything?

> *(Monty shrugs.)*

CHAP: The food?

> *(Monty shrugs.)*

CHAP: She tells me you haven't been eating much.

> *(Monty shrugs.)*

CHAP: She said you're wearing out the carpet, as well.

> *(Monty immediately looks down.)*

CHAP: There's a lot of room here, brother. Lots of room.

> *(A short beat.)*

MONTY: Why are you here again?

CHAP: I told you, I was in the—

CHAP:	MONTY:
—neighborhood.	In the neighborhood. Yeah, yeah, you said that.

CHAP: I was.

MONTY: You live in Bensonhurst, now?

CHAP: All I did is drop in to say hello. I can go, if you'd like.

MONTY: No. You don't have to go.

CHAP: . . .

MONTY: It's just. You're watching me like Liz.

CHAP: How is that?

MONTY: Like, waiting. Expecting me to say something.

CHAP: How does that make you feel?

(Both men smile. Monty gives Chap the finger.)

CHAP: Have you asked her what she's expecting you to say?

MONTY: No.

CHAP: Maybe you should.

(A short beat.)

MONTY: You do this with everyone? Or is this, you know, some kind of official check in?

CHAP: No. It's not an official check in. This isn't part of my job.

MONTY: But it's a check in.

CHAP: It's not a check in.

MONTY: What is it, then?

CHAP: I wanted to see how you were doing.

MONTY: A check in.

CHAP: A friendly chat. We're friends, right? And isn't that what friends do? Have friendly chats?

MONTY: I guess.

CHAP: Then that's why I'm here.

MONTY: As long as you don't expect me to say anything.

CHAP: No, I learned that lesson. Took me a number of years, but I learned it.

(Monty smiles. A short beat.)

MONTY: Do you ever talk to WoJo?

CHAP: Once in a while. If I see him around.

MONTY: If you could ask him, how's the puppy?

CHAP: Puppy? She's gotta be, what, six or seven by now?

MONTY: Seven. If you could find out?

CHAP: I'll find out.

(A short beat.)

MONTY: Laura Chapman sent me a letter.

CHAP: I know. She contacted me as well.

MONTY: Is that why you came?

CHAP: Absolutely not. If I may ask, what did you do with it?

MONTY: Return to Sender.

CHAP: You may want to consider talking to her at some point. Because—if I may—I think it's important that—

MONTY: Anything else? Any other paperwork or loose ends that they sent you to take care of? Because they already talked to me about the other thing, and I told them I don't care.

(A short beat.)

CHAP: No one sent me here, Monty.

MONTY: . . .

CHAP: What's going on with you?

MONTY: I'm tired.

CHAP: I'm tired, too. You're not sleeping?

MONTY: What about sleepwalking?

(A short beat.).

CHAP: Sleepwalking.

MONTY: Yes. Does it mean something?

CHAP: It could. You tell me.

MONTY: I mean . . . Uh . . . Yeah . . . There's . . . You know.

(Monty looks at the floor.)

MONTY: Before I went to sleep the other night—my first night, you know—I started thinking about . . . How . . . Just, you know . . . Fucked. All of this is. Just—just—just—Everything. Fucked. I have nothing.

CHAP: Monty—

MONTY: No, it's the truth. I have nothing. No skills. No job. No family—I mean, there's my sister, but—yeah. No, whatever, wife or girlfriend or kids who were waiting for me—no family of my own. And I fell asleep. Thinking of that. The nothingness.

(A short beat.)

And I woke up, and—and—and—I woke up and I'm in my sister's car. In the garage. Behind the wheel. And—and—

and—the engine is running. And. It's. Just. Yeah. It's hard to breathe. And I wake up and. Yeah. I wake up and think *'Fuck it.'*
(Chap leans forward, hand over his mouth. Silence. A short beat. Monty smiles.)
And I'm totally fucking with you right now. Sorry.
(Chap stares at him. Silence. He rises.)

CHAP: This was a mistake.

MONTY: I'm sorry.

CHAP: No, you're right. I shouldn't have come here. I didn't mean to waste your time. Or mine. There are actually people who want to talk to me. Who need to talk to me. I don't have to come here. I probably shouldn't come here. So I'm going to go. Because this—

CHAP:	MONTY:
—is horse shit	I'm sorry. I
Monty. It's horse	shouldn't—

shit.

MONTY: I'm sorry.

CHAP: *(cracking a smile)* And I'm totally fucking with you right now.
They laugh.

CHAP: Oh, that feels good. It's good to see you. Sleepwalking . . .
(Monty smiles. A short beat.)

MONTY: Just now? Liz asked me to go to the store. It's nice out. So I figured I would take a little walk. And I was crossing—about to cross—the street. And the little 'walk' guy comes on and I start to cross and I can't move. I'm just. Yeah. Stuck. Just . . . There. My legs won't move and the people behind me are bumping into me and yelling at me and calling me names but. Yeah. And then the light starts blinking red and then the little hand comes on and. And. Yeah. I think, 'If I run now, I can make it.' But I don't. I. Can't? Can't. Stupid, you know? I couldn't. Can't. Cross the street. And this guy behind me yells, "Walk, you fucken' idiot!" And I did. And. Yeah. I don't even know how to walk any more without someone telling me.

(Chap stares at Monty, who looks up at him. A very long beat.)
MONTY wasn't joking that time.
CHAP: I know.

ASUNCION

Jesse Eisenberg

Comic
Edgar, twenties
Vinny, thirties

> *Edgar and Vinny share an apartment. Well, it's Vinny's apartment and basically Edgar crashes on the floor. Vinny teaches at a local college, and Edgar is a former student. Edgar fancies himself an investigative journalist and is fascinated by Asuncion, a young Filipino woman recently married to his brother Stuart, who has parked Asuncion with Edgar and Vinny for a few days, for some mysterious reason. Edgar has become convinced that Asuncion is actually a sex slave. This just might be the Big Story he's been looking for.*

EDGAR: We gotta get her out of here.

VINNY: What?

EDGAR: Or maybe we should get out of here and call the police.

VINNY: What the hell are you talking about?

EDGAR: Okay, Vinny, I think—and just hear me out here—but I think she might be a sex slave.

VINNY: Excuse me?

EDGAR: It's not clear to you?

VINNY: What's not clear?

EDGAR: All the clues!

VINNY: Dude, what clues?

EDGAR: She is from the Philippines, Vinny! You're practically born into the sex trade there if you're not from fucking white European colonial descent.

VINNY: I'm sure there are women from the Philippines who are not sex slaves.

EDGAR: Yeah? Name one! He's probably hiding her out here! Homeland security is probably on to them and that's why he wouldn't tell us what's going on! It's all starting to gel.

VINNY: Calm down! What did he tell you? Did he say where they met?

EDGAR: Yes! On the internet! And I've been to these websites, for my work. You go online, there are thousands of pictures of young girls. Remember I wrote that article, *The Meat Market of Europe* about Ukraine? Well the Philippines is the same thing, but with Asians.

VINNY: I don't think Stuart would do that.

EDGAR: Stuart is *exactly* the kind of guy who does shit like this. He lost his virginity to a prostitute in Red Bank.

VINNY: He did?

EDGAR: Yes, on prom night.

VINNY: I didn't know that. Either way you're an idiot. Look, if you think she's a sex worker, just ask her.

EDGAR: No! You can't ask a victim about their oppressor. They're brainwashed to worship them and lie. We have to be very gentle with her. And when Stuart returns on Monday, we hide Asuncion, call the police from the bathroom and have Stuart arrested.

VINNY: So she can stay until Monday?

EDGAR: Yes, until I sort out what to do.

VINNY: Good, she's kind of hot.

EDGAR: Vinny! Don't say that! Don't sexualize her!

VINNY: Why not? She is.

EDGAR: She's not for that kind of consumption. She's to be pitied! She's a victim, she's a sex slave victim!

VINNY: Well if she is it's because she's hot.

EDGAR: Vinny!

VINNY: Don't feel so guilty Edgar. Women like her, if she is a *sex worker*—and don't say slaves—they think of sex differently. They've been trained to do it to please the man rather than receive pleasure themselves so it's thought of like a service, rather than as recreation.

EDGAR: No no—Sex should be a mutually enjoyable experience. If it has to be had.

VINNY: So should skiing. Which you hate. But when your fat little girlfriend wanted to go skiing last year, you went with her, because you were fucking her and it was worth it. Sometimes two people do things that one of them enjoys more.

EDGAR: Huh. That's not a bad point.

VINNY: Fuck you, don't condescend.

EDGAR: Sorry.

VINNY: This is interesting. Let's travel down this garden path for a minute. A sex worker might be in our house. And a sex worker's duty is to please the man of the house. Which, in this case, is so obviously me. In fact, I think I may take her skiing.

EDGAR: Vinny! She's my brother's wife!

VINNY: She's staying in my apartment. Quid pro quo.

EDGAR: Vinny, please . . .

VINNY: You may want to hit the slopes yourself young Eddie!

EDGAR: This is absurd! I can't tell if you're joking!

VINNY: Me neither.

EDGAR: She's my sister!

VINNY: She's not your sister! And you haven't had sex for a year. It's not healthy Edgar.

EDGAR: Stop talking like this, it's disgusting. *(intimately)* It's been more than a year. I haven't masturbated in 3 months.

VINNY: Jesus, Edgar! Don't tell me that!

EDGAR: The last time I masturbated, I did for five hours. Five hours, One ejaculation. I hated myself for one week after that. I couldn't look in a mirror. I couldn't look at my naked body. I dressed at night in the dark and slept in my clothes and wore them the next day so I wouldn't ever see me. And my penis was smaller than ever. It was like it was dried and bagged. Like NASA ice cream or a shriveled apricot that occasionally pissed.

VINNY: *(gently)* You're unhealthy, buddy.

EDGAR: I used to be inspired.

VINNY: *(laughing)* You should cure yourself by having sex with your sister, Edgar. *(Edgar laughs too)* Actually, what you should do, Edgar, *what you should do*—You should write a story about her.

EDGAR: Huh . . .

VINNY: While she's here. You should write a story about her, about her *plight*. A personal account of Asuncion, an orphan child born on the streets of Calcutta—or wherever she's from, you can work out the details on your own—and hidden in the hull of a steamer, gnawing on the fallen breadcrumbs from her master's supper, and traversing the seven seas just to marry your dumb brother.

EDGAR: That's actually a great idea.

VINNY: You could be published!

EDGAR: You think?

VINNY: And then pay me some rent.

EDGAR: The Nation would take something like this—

VINNY: Even Vanity Fair—

EDGAR: I could win a Pulitzer!

VINNY: I don't think you'll win a Pulitzer.

EDGAR: Well, you said Vanity Fair, so I was just going along with the dream—

VINNY: It's good to have dreams, Edgar.

EDGAR: But you can't tell her what I'm doing.

VINNY: Don't tell me what to do.

EDGAR: Oh right, sorry.

VINNY: And don't apologize.

EDGAR: Okay sor—Okay. I could call it *A Woman In The Shadows*. No no . . . *Out from the Shadows*.

VINNY: What about . . . *The Pacific Rim-job*.

EDGAR: That's good—that's funny. What about *Stopped Traffick*?

VINNY: *The Great Barrier Queef!*

EDGAR: I'm going to write something so great, Vinny. I'm going to save her!

Information on this playwright may be found at www.smithandkraus.com. Click on the AUTHORS tab

CQ/CX

Gabe McKinley

Dramatic
Jay, twenties, African American
Gerald, fifties, African American

Jay, a young reporter at the New York Times, is summoned by his superior and sometimes mentor Gerald to face a plagiarism accusation, a charge that incites them both to examine their relationship and how they fit at the newspaper.

Gerald's office. Gerald sits across from Jay. A short silence.

GERALD: Jay.

JAY: I've talked to Jim about this . . . and . . .

GERALD: Jay, I've been on the phone with Robert Rivard, the executive editor of the San Antonio Express. He called seeing if I wanted to thank him.

JAY: For what?

GERALD: He wanted me to thank him for having his reporter write a story for the New York Times.

JAY: I told Jim what must have happened.

GERALD: Howard Kurtz is running a story in tomorrow's Washington Post detailing the similarities between your story and Monica's. This is serious, Jay.

JAY: I understand that . . . .Her story got mixed in with my notes. I must've . . . I must've . . .

GERALD: This is serious, Jay.

JAY: I know . . . There are cases where this has happened before, I looked it up . . . This Baltimore Sun columnist . . .

GERALD: Jay, you know we protect our reporters.

JAY: Well, I don't feel protected right now.

GERALD: But we need your cooperation.

JAY: Cooperation? I told you, her story . . . my notes . . . I just . . .

GERALD: We need proof that you where in Los Fresnos.

JAY: What? Of course I was. What is this?

GERALD: We need receipts. The hotel, the rental car . . .

JAY: Okay. Okay. My credit cards are maxed and I had to sleep in my car. It's embarrassing. I told Jim about the rental car, ask him.

GERALD: They don't have you on record as renting a car.

JAY: Then I told you the wrong place. I'll go and I'll get them.

GERALD: Sit down.

JAY: Let me just go home and review the . . . . I was there Gerald. This is starting to piss me off.

GERALD: The family, this mother Rosa Arenas, doesn't remember talking to you. She's talked to a lot of press, but she doesn't remember someone from the Times.

JAY: She's wrong.

GERALD: Jay. Listen to me. This is the situation. This is happening, brother. If you want us to protect you, we need proof. Hard evidence. People are saying..

JAY: What? I didn't do anything wrong.

GERALD: Something is amiss, Jay.

JAY: Are you going to suspend me?

GERALD: You're gonna be suspended at a minimum, Jay. I don't think you're listening.

 JAY: I am.

GERALD: Then talk to me. Tell me the truth.

JAY: The truth is . . . I work for the New York Times, I'm a writer for the New York Times. I'm a newspaper writer, Gerald. It's in my blood . . . it's . . . who I am. So, to insinuate . . . it's offensive. I have done everything this place has asked me to do . . . and maybe it has eaten me up a little . . . maybe I've given too much . . . I need a little rest. I've been around these families, these families that have been blown up by the war . . . crying mothers and fathers, who when you look into their eyes you see no light, just this absence of . . . anything, like dark empty rooms. I have to look into their eyes and say, "what does it feel like?" What does is feel like to have your son or daughter die this terrible way, and "who do you blame?" And please don't take too long to articulate it, because I have a seven-thirty deadline, and then I have to file my expenses . . . plus I gotta get out of town tomorrow to talk to another family, push my way into their living room and ask them the same goddamn questions.

GERALD: I understand the pressure. But that is the job.

JAY: All I ever wanted to do was write for this paper, my whole life . . . and it happened. Do you know what that feels like? To be hurt by something you love. To hurt something you . . . Do you understand? *(Beat)* Now you? Not you. To be scorned. I love this place . . . it's my home.

GERALD: I do understand. I've given my entire adult life to this paper . . . my first marriage, a woman I loved very much, I gave her up for this place. I understand, Jay. See? But you have to understand, that if you love this place you have to tell me how deep this goes. It's not just a newspaper, Jay. It's a symbol, and idea . . . It's the truth . . . It is a public trust . . . and once that trust is shattered, it will never come back, unless we're totally forthright about what happened. Do you understand? If you can't trust a newspaper, it becomes useless. Help me. Please, Jay . . .

JAY: What do you want to hear? Yes. I made mistakes.

GERALD: Mistakes?

JAY: Yes.

GERALD: Plural. More than one? Are there others? How many?

JAY: I don't know. Mistakes were made.

GERALD: How many mistakes, Jay? Is this isolated? This looks bad. You don't have a lot of friends around here right now. Just help us sort this out. Is this a one time thing? Jay, are you listening? Look at me . . . is it?

JAY: One time thing? We're friends? Right? Still?

GERALD: This is an office, and I am your superior. I care about you, like I care about all these people who I work with.

JAY: I was special though. I wrote about you, I nominated you for that award, I bragged about you.

GERALD: I never asked for any of that.

JAY: But, I did anyway. So, you'd like me..so you'd. Fuck. What did they tell you?

GERALD: I'm sorry?

JAY: Go get that runaway slave. Bring him home. Is that what they said. Gerald, you're black, reel that nigger in . . . brother to brother.

GERALD: Brother to brother? You wanna talk brother to brother? Do you realize what this could mean? Brother to brother. What it'll mean for . . .

JAY: Come on, Uganda X . . .

GERALD: We have to be better. You never understood that, or I didn't make it clear. This. Whatever it is . . . will destroy everything we have worked for . . . everything . . . It'll bring us all down.

JAY: You know what they call you and Hal? Huck Finn and Nigger Jim.

GERALD: Race—me and you, what we are—shouldn't have anything to do with this.

JAY: But it will. Isn't that the story . . . What's the story, Gerald? If you were writing it . . . what would you lead with?

GERALD: You tell me.

JAY: A young New York Times reporter . . . No. A brilliant young New York Times reporter . . .

GERALD: You're burying your lead.

JAY: A brilliant young New York Times reporter . . . made a mistake . . . he . . . he . . . Stop. Don't you see what these people are trying to do? Trying to divide us. Father versus son.

GERALD: I'm not your father, Jay . . .

JAY: He died in Vietnam.

GERALD: I thought he worked for the Pentagon?

JAY: Yeah. I mean, no. Should I get a lawyer?

GERALD: No. The truth. Tell me!

JAY: Don't yell at me!

GERALD: I'm sorry. The cardinal rule, Jay. Did you fabricate, did you steal? Tell me . . . tell me. It'll be alright. I promise. But we have to start with the truth.

JAY: It'll be alright? You promise? I'll still have a job, no matter what?

GERALD: Jay, I can't promise that.

JAY: Promise.

GERALD: I can't do that, Jay. You know that.

JAY: Promise me, you'll still be my friend.

GERALD: I'm still your friend. But that means you're my friend . . . my friends tell me their secrets.

JAY: You said you'd be watching me. I wanted you to be proud of me.

GERALD: Maybe I did look at you and see something familiar. A distant . . .

JAY: What?

GERALD: I'm guilty of that. God know. I don't know how I'm going to live with . . . But now is not the time to dwell . . . We'll go through every story you ever wrote, Jay. We'll find out. Just make it easier.

JAY: You're right. You're not my father. You're my uncle Tom.

GERALD: Jay,

JAY: I'll resign, then you won't be able to make me do anything. I'll write a book. A book about this place. I know where all the bodies are buried.

GERALD: No. We are going to sit here and figure this out.

JAY: This interview is over. You'll have my resignation shortly.

GERALD: Jay. Don't do this.

JAY: It is going to make a great story, Gerald. It is going to make a great story.

(Jay exits.)

ELECTRA

Don Nigro

Dramatic
Thomas Ryan, twenty-seven
Nick Demetrius, forty

Scene: A swing on the front porch of the Ryan house in Armit-age, a small town in east Ohio.
Time: 1920
Thomas Ryan comes home from World War I after being thought dead, and is told by his sister Lexie that it wasn't in the bathtub, but instead their mother, Carolyn, who has ac-cused Jenna and allowed her to be put in a mental institution. Lexie says Carolyn has been having an affair with Jenna's husband Nick, who got into the family in the first place by blackmailing Thomas's father about a murder in New York years ago. Now Nick works at his father in law's bank and drinks. He loves both Jenna and Lexie, but has slipped into an affair with their mother largely out of loneliness, guilt and despair. Carolyn scares him. As a boy, Thomas looked up to Nick, wanted to be like him, and felt unloved by his preoc-cupied father and difficult mother. Now Thomas is trying to decide what to do. He is sick of killing, and is suffering from serious mental trauma from his experiences in the war. He doesn't know whether to believe Lexie's stories or not. Lexie insists that he must help her kill both their mother and Nick, since the local Sheriff is corrupt and stupid and will do noth-ing. Thomas is sitting on the porch swing, trying to decide what to do. Nick has been sent out by the suspicious Carolyn to find out what Thomas is up to.

THOMAS: Fireflies. Ocean of darkness. Everything resolves itself into yes, no, and maybe. The present is yes, the past is no, the future is maybe. Life is yes, death is no, and love is maybe. They gave me a medal because I got confused and retreated towards the enemy. Going round in circles like the mill horse. The dead men had letters on them. Scattered about in the mud. Splattered with blood and brains and excrement. Two Dutch girls in a room full of strawberries and ticking clocks.

NICK: *(Coming out onto the porch, with flask.)* Who are you talking to out here?

THOMAS: The air is saturated with flying creatures. Lightning bugs are the souls of the dead.

NICK: Buddy, you sound like a man who needs a drink.

THOMAS: I don't drink.

NICK: Well, if you're going to live in this house, you'd damn well better learn.

(Sitting down beside Thomas and giving him the flask.)

Go on. It'll kill you, but slowly. Like a woman.

THOMAS: I don't like to drink. It makes me somebody else.

NICK: I wish it did that for me.

THOMAS: I have enough trouble behaving decently when I'm sober.

NICK: I don't have that problem. I never behave decently. And I'm never sober.

THOMAS: What's happened to you?

NICK: Too much of the wrong kind of thing.

THOMAS: I looked up to you when I was a boy.

NICK: Well, you were short then. You've grown considerably. Now you can gaze down upon me as if from a great height. Of course, who can't?

THOMAS: I loved my father but I couldn't talk to him. He was always thinking about something else. You were the person I wanted to be.

NICK: Yes, I see myself as a role model for the youth of America. I'm proud of my accomplishments. What are they again?

THOMAS: It was partly the combination of charm and assurance you had. I'll never have that. I'll always make women uneasy. I can see it in their eyes.

NICK: Never look a woman in the eyes. Fatal mistake. Not the eyes. Not the breasts. Focus on her eyebrows.

THOMAS: In Paris I went backstage at a theatre once. Some other soldiers were standing with some of the performers, watching the next act playing from the wings. One of the actresses watching with them was naked from the waist up.

She was perfectly comfortable with the others. Not shy at all. But when her eyes met mine, she immediately covered herself and went back in her dressing room. Now why did she do that? All those other soldiers there, and she was fine with them. What was it about me that suddenly made her feel naked?

NICK: Women like to be looked at. They just don't want you to see anything. You have the look of a saint who's just ripped his palms down off a cross.

(Nick drinks.)

THOMAS: Lexie says you never go see Jenna.

NICK: Jenna doesn't want to see me.

THOMAS: She's your wife.

NICK: Which would tend to explain why she doesn't want to see me.

THOMAS: It might help her if you'd go and talk with her once in a while. Just spend some time with her.

NICK: I can't. I couldn't look her in the eye.

THOMAS: I don't understand what's the matter with you people. Why can't anybody here just try and behave like a decent, normal person for once?

NICK: There are no decent, normal people. Nobody decent is normal. And nobody normal is decent. The only decent, normal people are the dead. So. How do you like being home so far?

THOMAS: Have you ever considered suicide?

NICK: Every night of my life.

THOMAS: I'm serious.

NICK: So am I. But on the whole I seem to prefer, inexplicably, the cowardice of continuing to live. Have you considered it?

THOMAS: Yes.

NICK: Maybe you should take Lexie and get the hell out of this place.

THOMAS: Take Lexie where?

NICK: I don't know. Anywhere. Just not here.

THOMAS: You'd be more comfortable if we were gone, would you?

NICK: I'd be more comfortable if everybody was gone, including me.

THOMAS: Lexie wouldn't go.

NICK: Then go yourself. Just pack up and get out. If you need money, I can embezzle something for you from the bank.

THOMAS: I don't think I can.

NICK: Why not? What's keeping you here?

THOMAS: It feels like there's something I've got to do.

NICK: Really? What is it?

THOMAS: I'm still deciding.

(pause)

NICK: Well, be careful of your mother.

THOMAS: What do you mean?

NICK: Just watch out, is all. Your mother is not entirely in her right mind. I know that's not exactly a news bulletin, but while you've been gone she's managed to achieve a whole new level of dementia. Just be careful. I have no idea what she's capable of. Of course, I have no ideas of any sort. When one has descended this deeply into the abyss of carnivorous mythology, it becomes increasingly impossible to claw your way out. And whatever you choose to do—

(Flapping noises above.)

Jesus. What was that? Did you see that?

THOMAS: Yes.

NICK: What the hell was it?

THOMAS: What if you don't make choices?

NICK: What do you mean?

THOMAS: What if the choices are making you?

(Nick looks at him. The light fades on them.)

FIND AND SIGN

Wendy McLeod

Comic
Iago, thirties
Andrew, forties. Jamaican

> *Iago is the only white guy working at Freeman Records. His friend and boss Andre, 40's, originally from Jamaica, is likely to be taking over the entire label soon. Iago is angling for Andre's job, elbowing aside Cal, his competition, an African-American colleague. This scene takes place at a party in Tribeca, a trendy Manhattan neighborhood. Right before the scene begins, Iago had a flirtatious conversation with a woman he met at the party, named Julia.*

ANDRE: Who was that?

IAGO: That was Julia.

ANDRE: Pretty.

IAGO: She's a type.

ANDRE: Ouch.

IAGO: Smart. Bohemian. Sassy.

ANDRE: What's wrong with all that?

IAGO: She told me I was sexy.

ANDRE: Then what you doing here?

IAGO: The night is young.

ANDRE: Go. What's the worst that can happen? You feel something.

IAGO: You know what makes me sad? The stuffed animals on the bed.

ANDRE: Whose bed?

IAGO: The women at the parties. Inside, they're still little girls. And there you are with the condom you tucked in your wallet before you even met them.
(Andre sees the beautiful model that has been in Iago's sights for some time.)

ANDRE: Jesus.

IAGO: I know.

ANDRE: What do you call that? That thing's she's wearing?

IAGO: I don't know but that shit is better than naked.

ANDRE: Tunic? Caftan?

IAGO: It's like wearing smoke.

ANDRE: Can those be real?

IAGO: That, my friend, is the buoyancy of youth.

ANDRE: Another beer?

IAGO: I'll go.

ANDRE: I'll bet you will.

IAGO: But first I've got to ask you something. Rumor has it . . .

ANDRE: Steve's getting married, he's not leaving the label . . .

IAGO: I hear . . .

ANDRE: He's getting married!

IAGO: The fiancee works for the Asia Foundation and they're moving to Singapore . . .

ANDRE: We're at a party.

IAGO: You know and I know that's where business is done.

ANDRE: I'm speaking now of boundaries . . .

IAGO: If Steve leaves, who's taking over the label? You are.

ANDRE: Not necessarily.

IAGO: Of course you are.

ANDRE: They bring people in all the time.

IAGO: Who would they bring in?

ANDRE: Somebody younger. Somebody "street."

IAGO: Oh c'mon, when Steve leaves, you're taking over . . .

ANDRE: Assuming there's still a label to run . . .

IAGO: We had a great year last year . . .

ANDRE: But how much longer will there be labels?

IAGO: Maybe Lady Gaga doesn't need a label, but new artists need a label! And when you move up, who's going to run the A and R department? You know and I know it comes down to Cal or me. Hear me out. In our business, it all goes down at the clubs and the parties and the after-parties and where is Cal tonight?

ANDRE: I have no idea . . .

IAGO: Cal is at a baby shower . . .

ANDRE: Theirs?

IAGO: That would require sperm count. No, he's off at a friend's baby shower, and do you know what he's bringing?

ANDRE: You mean the actual present or the one you're making up to make Cal look like a pussy . . . ?

IAGO: I don't have to make him look like a pussy. I'll leave it at this. A Boppy.

ANDRE: What's a Boppy?

IAGO: Exactly.

ANDRE: No, seriously. What's a Boppy?

IAGO: What comes to mind?

ANDRE: Like a . . . punching bag clown?

IAGO: No, that would be fun. A Boppy is a nursing pillow.

ANDRE: I don't get it.

IAGO: It wraps around the woman's post-partum belly, allowing the child access to the nibs, not unlike the phone books they will later sit on to reach the dinner table.

ANDRE: Is that a good present?

IAGO: I don't know! I don't have children! I don't have a wife! I don't have a girlfriend! You know what I have? A job! You know what gets all my time? My job. You know what I dream about? My job . . .

ANDRE: Look, man, you want some career advice? You should have a life. You should have a girlfriend. At your age, you should have a fiancee.

IAGO: You're not engaged!

ANDRE: But I want to be!

IAGO: You want to be engaged in the abstract, what you have is this fantasy of being engaged . . .

ANDRE: That's how things begin . . . .

IAGO: Except when it's real, you go to kiss her and she's got morning breath. You see the mother in the muumuu, the father with the comb-over. You've got to deal with, whatever, the A.D.D. brother or the dad's electric trains.

ANDRE: Aren't one-night stands horrible in their own way?

IAGO: If they are, it's one night. If a marriage is horrible it's every night.

ANDRE: You have no template of a happy marriage . . .

IAGO: Don't give me that . . .

ANDRE: Your mother, correct me if I'm wrong, was a single mother . . .

IAGO: Surely this is not such an anomaly . . .

ANDRE: In the black community?

IAGO: In any community! Are you not going to promote me because you think I'm a racist?

ANDRE: I don't think you're a racist. I know you're a racist.

IAGO: How long have we been friends?

ANDRE: "Some of my best friends are black."

IAGO: Some of my best friends are black.

ANDRE: One of your best friends is black.

IAGO: Do you really think I'm racist?

ANDRE: No more so than any other white guy . . .

IAGO: That is a racist thing to say. "All white people are racist." That's racist!

ANDRE: Spare me the forensics . . .

IAGO: Nobody knows more about hip-hop than I do! Go on. Sing something. I'll name the act. I'll name the label. I'll name every album they've ever made.

ANDRE: This perpetual adolescence, man, it's not attractive. You don't want to be that guy with the grey ponytail buying drinks for the teen-age models . . . .

IAGO: Please. This is a two-hundred dollar haircut.

ANDRE: That is?

IAGO: *(smiling)* Fuck you.
(Iago starts across the room towards the bar and the caftan girl Andre stops him.)

ANDRE: It's time to settle down, my brother.

HESPERIA

Randall Colburn

Seriocomic
Trick, twenty-five
Ian, twenty-eight

Ian's porn film career has tanked and he's come home for the wedding of his childhood best friend Claudia, a former porn star and his former lover, and Trick, a youth minister, who went to a neighboring high school though they weren't friends.

TRICK: Stur-*man*. Trick-Stur-Man.

IAN: Trickster Man. Trick.

TRICK: The kids seem to like it.

IAN: Is that what you prefer?

TRICK: If you like. It's kind of a staple around here.

IAN: I'm just Ian. Not much you can do with Ian Kreiger (*Kree-ger*)

TRICK: Maybe "Blitz"-Kreiger.

IAN: That's good.

TRICK: Sorry. Nerd alert, I know. *(Trick laughs. It dies out.)* I, um, I just want you to know that your lifestyle doesn't bother me.

IAN: Likewise.

TRICK: Good.

IAN: But things change, huh? Just trying to, like, figure things out now.

TRICK: Well, that's the first step, huh? Figuring out how to figure things out.
     (…)
Must be nice being around your old stomping grounds, huh? You grew up in Lawson, yeah?

IAN: Yeah, both of us.

TRICK: She's told me a little about you.

IAN: She's told me nothing about you.

TRICK: Well, I teach at Hesperia Elementary, my alma mater, third grade. I also head the youth group at HCC.

IAN: So you grew up here?

TRICK: Born and raised, yep. My dad, my dad's dad, so on…

IAN: This was the one place we never went. I mean, grew up in Lawson, partied in Lightley, ran track in Nickelville, rode our bikes to Concordia, to Coulter. But Hesperia… never went to Hesperia. Never once. Only saw the steeple in the distance.

TRICK: You ran track?

IAN: Sure.

TRICK: Me, too. And we had our meets in Nickelville—didn't have a track at the high school.

IAN: How old are you?

TRICK: 25.

IAN: I think I remember you. You would've been a freshman when I was a senior but you ran the hurdles. They used to say, "Rev it, Trev!" when you'd near the finish.

TRICK: (laughing) They did!

IAN: No shit, I remember that. *(A moment.)* Sorry—

TRICK: (a smile) No, it's okay, really. Express yourself.

IAN: Who knows?

TRICK: Who knows . . . ?

IAN: Who here knows . . . about her?

TRICK: Just Pastor Bolt and I. When she's ready she'll tell the rest of the congregation.

IAN: Okay.

(Ian looks around.)

Thanks for this, letting me stay. I gotta sort some things out before I head out east. I've got some people out there, and like…

(He sort of trails off. A moment.)

TRICK: She's happy you're here.

(…)

She never disregarded your significance, Ian.

(IAN nods, not looking at him.)

Scary as it can be, it's important to confront every aspect of our lives, to integrate every layer into our being. Claudia understands that. It was a, well, a *long road* these last few years. But she's forgiven herself.

IAN: Yeah, well, I guess there's plenty to be sorry about, huh?

(A moment. Looking at Trick)

How did you guys meet?

TRICK: Church social, actually. She was brand new in town.

IAN: And you started dating.

TRICK: No, no, we were friends for a long time. She didn't come here looking for anything but God. That was a draw to me, that steadfastness. That she was looking for something she didn't understand. There's bravery in that.

IAN: Yeah, totally.

TRICK: Totally.

IAN: *Totally.*

(A mildly awkward moment. Trick puts a hand on his shoulder.)

TRICK: Really, Ian, I know you're coming from a tough place. You stay as long as you like.

IAN: But the wedding—

TRICK: She would want you there.

IAN: Really?

TRICK: Totally. *(He looks Trick in the eyes.)* Also, if you're interested, I mean…we would *love* for you to come to service on Sunday.

IAN: I don't know, man.

TRICK: You'll be my guest. See, I'm kind of a big deal over there.

(Ian doesn't want to, but He laughs. Trick joins him.)

IAN: I really wanted you to be an asshole.

(They laugh harder.)

Home of the Great Pecan

Stephen Bittrich

Comic
Sheriff Bart, fifties to sixties
Diggity, mid to late twenties

> *Sunday morning in the sleepy town of Seguin, Texas, and Sheriff Bart is snoozing in his well-worn office chair before the official start of the work day and is rudely awoken by his over-eager young deputy Diggity, who brings him devastating news: the beloved Great Pecan, a huge quarter ton statue which is the very symbol of the town's greatest resource as well as the focus of the yearly Pecan Festival (culminating in the crowning of the Pecan Queen) has been stolen. The determined Sheriff Bart promises to leave no nut unturned in the pursuit of the culprit.*

> *In the Court House Building downtown. Sheriff Bart is sleeping in his chair. His brand new Deputy, Diggity, comes bursting in. Diggity sports an awful toupee.*

DIGGITY: Sheriff. Sheriff Bart! C-C-Come quick. Uh, Uh, uh, you gotta—you gotta—

SHERIFF BART: *(Lurching out of his seat)* Jesus Christ Alive, Diggity, you tryin' to give me a heart attack?

DIGGITY: But—but—you gotta—you gotta—

SHERIFF BART: Boy, you wanna back out and try knockin' 'fore you come in?

DIGGITY: But you gotta come quick!

SHERIFF BART: I ain't *gotta* do nothing but pay taxes and die.

DIGGITY: We got a robbery on our hands.

SHERIFF BART: Now, now, hole on. Give it to me slow. You say we got some kinda robbery—?

DIGGITY: Outside.

SHERIFF BART: Outside is a mighty big place, boy.

DIGGITY: *(As if leading him to the spot)* Outside—outside the building. Uh, uh, down the stairs. Uh, uh, down the sidewalk—

SHERIFF BART: You gonna give me dee-rections, Diggity?

DIGGITY: The Great Pecan.

SHERIFF BART: Yeah, I'm there.

DIGGITY: Well, it ain't there.

SHERIFF BART: Say what?

DIGGITY: Somebody went'n took the Great Pecan.

SHERIFF BART: Took the Great—

DIGGITY: There ain't nothing left but the sign.

SHERIFF BART: That thang must weigh a good five hunert pound. It's pure concrete.

DIGGITY: Well, they stole it.

SHERIFF BART: You know who took it, boy?

DIGGITY: No sir. I just saw it gone on my way up here. I don't know how you coulda missed it. It looks naked out there now.

SHERIFF BART: I slep' in the office las' night. Well, whatta we waitin' for? Uh lessee, now I want you ta get out there on the double and get me some infomation on this deal. This is top priority right now. Don't say nothin' ta nobody yet—especially not ta Mayor Hoppe. He'll have a hissy fit.

DIGGITY: Where do I start?

SHERIFF BART: Well, start asking some of the store owners 'round the square—what time is it now?

DIGGITY: 6:30 in the am.

SHERIFF BART: Damn, boy! You crazy? What the hell you doin' here at 6:30 a.m.?

DIGGITY: I couldn't sleep. First day on the job and all.

SHERIFF BART: Diggity, Diggity, Diggity, you're like a woman at a white sale. Now calm yerself down.
(beat)
All right. Les' thank this out. That Pecan was there at 7:30 las' night cuz I chased a coupla juvenile delinquents off it las' night about that time. That means it happened sometime between yesterday evening and 6:30 this mornin' in the a.m. You know who hangs out there late at night is those criminal kids.
(beat)
I want you to go pick up...whas that boy's name—with the ear deal—hangs out with that girl—one whose sister

had that operation—cucumber got stuck—took her to the emergency room—doctor had that affair—whas' her name that cuts hair—beauty parlor on Guadalupe—next to the taco place—makes 'em real hot—gives ya flamin' diarrhea for three days—

DIGGITY: Chucky.

SHERIFF BART: Yeah, that's the kid. Pick him up.

DIGGITY: Sheriff Bart. There's—there's one other thang. It was dark out there.

SHERIFF BART: Gonna be dark 'til about seven, Diggity.

DIGGITY: Well, when I was driving up on Court Street, I saw some flashing lights and, and a saucerlike shape—

SHERIFF BART: Diggity, I really don't wanna hear this—

DIGGITY: I gotcha Sheriff, but with that report last Tuesday from Tammie Lynn—

SHERIFF BART: Tammie Lynn Schneider is an A-1 fruitcake, Diggity. Don't you start makin' like squirrel bate on me yer first day on the job.

DIGGITY: Well, I wouldn'ta thought too much of it, but there's these marks on the lawn out there right by the Pecan sign—kinda like circular burn marks—like some kinda circular flame shot down from above and—

SHERIFF BART: Diggity, I ain't none too cheery at 6:30 in the a.m. Takes me a pot of coffee, a breakfast taco, and about three hours 'fore I'm up. Don't be spoutin' off bullcrap ta piss me off 'fore I've had my breakfast taco!

DIGGITY: Sheriff, all I'm sayin' is—

SHERIFF BART: You go wake up Chucky and see what that little som-bitch has ta say fer hisself. I'll examine the sight isself. Now git.

DIGGITY: This is awful, Sheriff. The Pecan Festival started on Friday. What if we can't find it before the Pecan Parade? They won't be able to crown the Pecan Queen.
(wistfully)
My dear sweet Mamaw was Pecan Queen back in '47. It's a tradition that goes back a hunerd years.

SHERIFF BART: A hunerd and two, Diggity.

DIGGITY: Lord, this is a disaster.

SHERIFF BART: I'm gonna find that Pecan. Ain't nobody gonna take the Great Pecan out from under my nose and get away with it. Not on my watch. When I find out who did it, I won't jes throw the book, I'll pitch the whole damn library at 'im.

DIGGITY: *(He salutes.)* Yes, sir. *(He leaves.)*

SHERIF BART: Som-bitch.

Information on this playwright may be found at www.smithandkraus.com. Click on the AUTHORS tab

HURT VILLAGE

Katori Hall

Seriocomic
Buggy, mid to late twenties, African-American
Cornbread, mid to late twenties, African-American

Buggy is a soldier who has returned home from the Iraq War with a haunting secret. Cornbread, mixed-race or "high yella," is a FedEx employee and small-time drug dealer (also called "doughboy"). They are reconnecting after not having sen each other for a while. They begin talking about Cookie, a precocious 13 year-old girl who's a wannabe rapper.

CORNBREAD: She gettin' so big.

BUGGY: Yeah . . .

CORNBREAD: So, fuck witcha boy for a minute. What you been eatin'?

BUGGY: What *you* been eatin'?

CORNBREAD: I been eatin' real good since I got me a job on the "plantation."

BUGGY: Awww, damn maine.

CORNBREAD: Yeah, Fed Ex 'bout to have me throwin' my muthafuckin' back out. Liftin' they heavy-ass boxes. Makin' 5 dollars and a quarter on the hour.

BUGGY: Might as well be bent over pickin' cotton.

CORNBREAD: That what I know. But they the only ones hirin' niggahs wit a charge so . . . you know? Damn, niggah. It sho'll is good as hell to see you. Glad I got to see you fo' they move us all out.

BUGGY: Glad I came, too, hell. Y'all wun't gone tell nobody?

CORNBREAD: Hell, niggah, you the one done that stopped writin' folk, tellin' folk where you was at. We just thought the good ole boy was in heaven.

BUGGY: *(Looking around)* This some sad shit—

CORNBREAD: Ain't it? But I guess it's for the best. They, uh, gone flip these units. Memphis done got this thang—the

HOPE grant. 35 million to make these here units into"mix income" 'partments they sayin.' Hurt Village gone be turnt to Uptown Condos!

BUGGY: How dat gone work?

CORNBREAD: I dunno. Bougie ass niggahs don't like to stay nexta poor-ass niggahs, and white trash don't like to stay nexta niggahs, so how they gone brew that pot of stew, I don't know. They shoulda gave *me* that money, hmph. If you axe me, look like they tryin' to mix shit up that don't need mixin.' Just ask my ma and pop. Hell, I coulda told 'em that little recipe ain't gone work.

BUGGY: You always talkin' food.

CORNBREAD: Hell, I'm always hungry. Don't tell the missus, but, uhm, I done saved up enough money off that hustlin'... ...

BUGGY: Still on that track.

CORNBREAD: But, see I'ma 'bout to be out the game, bra. *This* the week I quit.

BUGGY: Yeah, niggah, whatever.

CORNBREAD: I'm fo' real! Playa, I'm workin' me a legit now. Fuck this shit. What Whitney Houston say? "Crack is whack!" The game ain't nothin' like it useta be. It useta be 'bout makin' a coupla dollars. Now, niggahs wanna kill ya' over a porch. I been doin' this shit e'er since high school. I'm tired, niggah. I asked God to let me hustle til' I made it and I done did it. Gone get me and homegirl a mansion out in Mississippi. As crazy as she is, maine. I swear fo' God, this my last week. Hell, tell ya what. You come in be my right hand man. The faster I sell it the faster I'm gone. I'll give you fifty straight off the prof.

(beat)

BUGGY: Niggah, I'm the protector of the United States. How I'ma be lookin' like slangin' rock on the porch?

CORNBREAD: 'Scuse me then ole-Ninja Turtle-lookin' ass warrior. Well, tell me about that war, then. You kilt some folks?

(beat)

BUGGY: Yeah.

CORNBREAD: You look like you done kilt 20 niggahs whitcho bare hands and shit. Look at you, maine. Ye'en like us, maine, you done did somethin' withcho life. Maine, make me 'bout to cry up in this bitch. I heard you been stationed all over the world. Germany, Philippines, hell, now, Iraq.

BUGGY: Yeah, my tour of duty over so . . .

CORNBREAD: You probably got so much action out there maine. Poppin' them Muslim maniacs in they head.

BUGGY: Nah, it wun' like that, really.

CORNBREAD: Maine, you went over there to free that country. That some brave ass shit. And I bet you can get pussy easy with that uniform.

BUGGY: *(Reluctant to divulge)* Well . . .

CORNBREAD: Don't tell me you been bumpin' some niggah booty?

BUGGY: Hell, nah!

CORNBREAD: Hell, niggah, well I ain't know! You ain't answering me skraight so I'm askin' ya is ya crooked.

BUGGY: *(Deepening his voice)* Hell, nah!

CORNBREAD: Just makin' sho'! It done got to be a epidemic down here. Now, I don't mind if a girl do that shit. That's sexy as hell. I went to the shake junt one night and saw two freaky deaks lookin for that chewin.' Hell, that's what I'm pursuin'. Lesbianos bes my favorito thingos, ye'en know? Toyia, know. We got some funny niggahs runnin' round out here, now. All out in the open. It's terrible.

BUGGY: Why you so concerned with it?

CORNBREAD: Hell, somebody gotta be! Somebody gotta make sho' folks livin' right, ya know what I'm sayin?

(Buggy nods his head.)

A solja. Done made it out. So to celebrate yo homecomin' we gone have to take the boys out to the shake junt. Take you on that Pure Passion trip, ya know what I'm sayin? Get you some pussy and some new tennie shoes cause it's tooooo hot for some boots. Welcome home, niggah.

Language Rooms

Jussef El Guindi

Dramatic
Ahmed, anywhere from his mid-twenties to early thirties
Nasser, anywhere from his mid-twenties to early thirties

In one of those so-called "Black Sites" run by the CIA, where renditioned terror suspects are sent to be interrogated, a Muslim American translator's loyalty begins to be questioned. One of the reason Ahmed's loyalty comes into question is due to the manner in which he conducted his last interrogation. His fellow translator, Nasser, felt he was expressing way too much empathy for the prisoner, Khaled. Knowing their standing among their CIA colleagues was already tenuous because of their religious faith, Nasser worries that a literal translation of what Ahmed said to Khaled might be interpreted as betraying unspoken sympathies for this fellow Muslim. So Nasser omits a few things when he translates Ahmed's interrogation for their supervisor. But Nasser's tampering with the translation of the interrogation only makes things worse with their supervisor, Kevin.

Locker room. (Nasser is at a table. He is taking socks out of a laundry basket and stuffing them with baseballs. There is a second box beside him. Also, there's a locker room bench with a towel on it. Ahmed steps into the room holding the Khaled case envelope.)

NASSER: Oh. —Hey.

AHMED: Hey.

NASSER: How, er . . . ? (seeing his expression) What happened?

AHMED: What happened?

NASSER: How did it go?

AHMED: How did what go?

NASSER: Your meeting with Kevin?

AHMED: Are you gonna repeat everything I say today?

AHMED: Yah, I think it's called vamping. In music. Improvising something until the real music kicks in. At which point everyone knows what the other one is playing at.

(Ahmed puts the envelope down on the table.)

NASSER: Is that the Khaled interrogation?

(Nasser picks up the envelope and opens it.)

AHMED: Not my interrogation. No. That's your interpretation of my interrogation. That's your translation of an interrogation that never took place.

NASSER: *(half to himself, looking over transcript)* Oh great. He didn't drop it.

AHMED: And that got me thinking . . . since you're the official transcriber. The only other Arabic speaker; the one who transcribes all my interviews, how many other interviews of mine have you mangled to a point where it reads like fiction.

NASSER: What did he say to you?

AHMED: Does it matter? You're holding the knife you stabbed me with.

NASSER: I didn't stab you, I was trying to save your ass. Did Kevin happen to mention *why* I changed the transcript? Why I ended up lying for you?

AHMED: So you admit it. Oh my God. *(then)* Wait a minute: Kevin knows? That you changed things?

NASSER: *Yes.* He called me in. He saw the tapes before I erased them. Heard enough of the English sections to know the transcripts I handed to him didn't match. Did he say why I felt I had to do that?

AHMED: When did this meeting take place?

NASSER: A couple of days ago.

AHMED: When?

NASSER: *A couple of days ago.*

AHMED: What the hell is going on?

NASSER: You screwed up! - With Khaled. - The interrogation. It went wrong so many ways I didn't know which end of the interrogation I should lie about. You want to know why there's this concern now about your "sympathies"? Your loyalty?

AHMED: *What?*

NASSER: What were you thinking when you said half the shit you did? Some new approach of incriminating yourself while trying to get information?

AHMED: *What?*

NASSER: The things you said. The questions you posed to make him admit things. You came off sounding like a coconspirator, the way you poured on the empathy and emotion

AHMED: Are we talking about the same interrogation?

NASSER: *(continuing)* When I transcribed it and saw how it sounded on paper, I knew exactly what they'd think. And what I needed to do to stop them from wondering about your loyalty. But then Kevin for some reason decided to watch the tapes before I erased them. Never has before. He heard the difference in the English sections and wanted to know what was up.

AHMED: Oh my God. You idiot.

NASSER: I know what you *thought* you were doing, getting chummy with Khaled, pretending to secretly be an admirer, telling him how honorable and just his cause was and how disgusting the Americans were acting.

AHMED: It was a tactic.

NASSER: No, that's what you think it was, but it didn't come off like that.

AHMED: It's a tactic, you *dick*! Gain their trust. Adopt their point of view, it's part of our manual!

NASSER: No no: the way you were doing it; the words you chose, it crossed the line, so many times.

AHMED: I don't believe this.

NASSER: And the passion in your voice, like you were finally expressing what you really felt and not just feigning sympathy. I can tell the difference with you.

AHMED: I came in here thinking you'd changed things to make me sound incompetent, an amateur, because you were threatened by me in case they have to make cut-backs.

NASSER: Threatened by you?

AHMED: And now I hear you say you were trying to *help* me?

NASSER: Threatened how? Your Arabic's a joke. Only I know how much of a buffoon you are when it comes to speaking the language.

AHMED: I know Arabic!

NASSER: You're as fluent as a jackass. That chump Hamid with the D.C. dog show was laughing at you. You hit the wall of your own language ignorance and then have to use force.

AHMED: And Khaled was about to confess why? Did I raise a hand? He was like a baby wanting to come into my arms because of my *skill* in persuading him of his *(makes quotation marks)*

"just cause", which in no way reflected what I thought, you sack of horse shit. Jesus Christ, this whole time, you've been trying to do me in.

NASSER: Fuck you, I may have hung myself because of you. Clearly Kevin's not dropping it like he said he would.

AHMED: Drop what? What am I being accused of?

(A sound from the shower stalls offstage. They turn in that direction.)

Is . . . is someone else here?

NASSER: (slight beat, moves to the stall) Not when I came in.

AHMED: Is that the shower?

NASSER: That's been busted and running all day.

AHMED: (coming up behind him) You see anyone?

NASSER: I can't see in the last stall. (to whoever might be in the shower stall) Hey!

(Ahmed grabs a sock from the table) Anyone in there? You jacking off in there, Bryan?

(Just before Nasser turns around, Ahmed wraps the sock around Nasser's neck and pulls.)

AHMED: Nasser: I have to say: I'm feeling a little betrayed.

NASSER: (choking) Achh.

AHMED: In fact, I'm feeling very underwhelmed by your friendship right now.

NASSER: (choking) Wai—.

AHMED: And I made such an effort with you. I said I don't have enough Muslim friends. I have to connect more. Take pride in my heritage.

NASSER: (choking) *Wait.*

AHMED: Now I find out you've been undermining me this entire time? You do want to be their top dog and cut me out. The language expert, the go-to Muslim.

NASSER: (choking) *Would you wait one minute!*

AHMED: What?

NASSER: (choking) Use the rope. Not the sock.

AHMED: What? (tries to shuffle himself and Ahmed to the box) Rope's in there. Use that. I'll hang on.

(Ahmed lets Nasser go. Nasser steps away from him, rubbing his neck.)

You are *such* a moron.—You see—you have to resort to force. And did it get results? Are you any wiser for it?

AHMED: I feel better for it, and I wasn't really trying.

NASSER: You *jerk.* I am trying to *help you.* I may have screwed things up, I admit it. Nothing like a cover up to make an initial screw-up seem worse. But I did it because I didn't want them to get any wrong ideas.

AHMED: My God: if he thinks my own buddy thinks I'm giving comfort and aide to the enemy, and, what? *Passing messages?*

NASSER: Listen to me. We're translators. Do you know what that is? That's one language skill and a beard trimmer away from the people they bring here. What separates us in their eyes is very little. I know you go on about how American you feel, but they don't see it that way. That's why I go overboard and act the back-slapping fool you take me for. You think I don't seethe when they make the jokes they do? Putting my mother and religion into the mix? We are who we translate to them. We can't put on the disguise of the enemy as a tactic *because we're already wearing it.* The language itself puts us in enemy territory.

AHMED: *You thought I was being sincere with Khaled? You thought I meant it?*

NASSER: Didn't you?—A little bit? As lunatic as some of these people are, we understand the mind-set. We get it. We're not so far removed from the people they bring here, as American as you might think you are.

AHMED: Maybe you.

NASSER: *(continuing)* Look me in the eye and tell me you didn't let a little of those feelings hang out in the Khaled interrogation. Just a little. One or two real feelings that wormed their way out.

(Ahmed stares at Nasser.)

AHMED: Wow . . . . You do want me to go down.

NASSER: You know what: Go to hell.

AHMED: You never did like having me around, did you?

NASSER: After what I risked for you? You ungrateful shit.

(Nasser impulsively picks up a nearby baseball bat.)

Go ahead, pick a sock. Any sock. I'll show you how I'll react this time.

AHMED: Bring it on, you two-faced bastard. You want to see what physical force really is.

(Ahmed grabs a sock with a ball in it.)

MICHAEL VON SIEBENBURG MELTS THROUGH THE FLOORBOARDS

Greg Kotis

Seriocomic
Sammy, twenties to thirties
Michael, thirties to forties

> *Michael von Siebenburg is a five hundred year old Austrian nobleman kept alive over the centuries by consuming a diet of specially tenderized, specially seasoned human flesh. Sammy also Austrian and ancient, is Michael's "Bagger," meaning he lures available, unsuspecting women into having a blind date with Michael - an encounter that leads to bad end for the date and a meal for Michael and Sammy. In this scene, Michael meets with Sammy on the loading dock of the building where Sammy works.*

> *Michael enters carrying something wrapped in butcher paper. He sits beside Sammy, placing the package between them.*

SAMMY: Success?

MICHAEL: A good date, Sammy, nice and clean.

SAMMY: No fighting?

MICHAEL: Not much.

SAMMY: Good, good. No fighting means no fear in the meat.

MICHAEL: She went down easy. Two glasses.

SAMMY: Nice and calm.

MICHAEL: Some anxiety, maybe, but no fear. Not that I could taste, anyway.

> *(Sammy picks up the package and weighs it in his hands.)*

SAMMY: So light.

MICHAEL: She was a professional woman, Sammy. The days of the fat farm girl are over.

> *(Sammy opens the package and takes out a pinch.)*

SAMMY: Just a taste.

> *(He eats a bite.)*

Mmmmm, yum. So good.

MICHAEL: Yes, the meat.

SAMMY: Didn't realize how hungry I was.

MICHAEL: A dry spell. Over for the moment.

SAMMY: Happy again.

MICHAEL: The meat.

SAMMY: The meat.

(Sammy bites deep into the meat, snurfling it down like a starving stray dog. Michael remains quiet as his friend satisfies himself. Finally)

You see "True Blood" last night?

MICHAEL: Tivo'd it.

SAMMY: Such lies.

MICHAEL: I know, you hate that show.

SAMMY: Yes, but it makes life easier for us. The lies.

MICHAEL: What's his name is good. The lead guy.

SAMMY: As if blood makes a meal, a full meal. Meat makes a meal! Specially tenderized, specially seasoned HUMAN MEAT!

MICHAEL: SSSHH!!

SAMMY: The meat. Such power. Like Sushi, but much, much more.

MICHAEL: Yes, but still, we must be careful.

(Sammy gobbles down some more . Then)

SAMMY: You want some?

MICHAEL: No. Thanks.

SAMMY: You sure? You look like you could use a piece of meat.

MICHAEL: I'm fine, Sammy, really.

SAMMY: You look tired, Michael, a little pale. Please, have a little piece of the meat.

MICHAEL: Not right now, Sammy. Thank you. Maybe later.

SAMMY: Not eat?

MICHAEL: What can I tell you? Sometimes we want to eat, sometimes we don't.

SAMMY: No, Michael, we always want to eat.

(beat)

MICHAEL: She came to me, Sammy. Last night. Around midnight.

SAMMY: She came to you?

MICHAEL: Last night. I was in bed, asleep, and she came to

me. She spoke my name.

SAMMY: I don't understand, Michael. Who came to you?

MICHAEL: Maria.

SAMMY: Maria?

MICHAEL: My wife Maria, from the old country.

SAMMY: Your wife Maria.

MICHAEL: Last night, around midnight.

(SAMMY considers this.)

SAMMY: You were dreaming.

MICHAEL: I wasn't dreaming.

SAMMY: It was late, you were sleeping. You had a bad dream.

MICHAEL: I'm telling you Sammy, this wasn't a dream. I could feel her there, I could smell the soil between her toes.

SAMMY: She's dead.

MICHAEL: I know she's dead.

SAMMY: Over five hundred years dead.

MICHAEL: I know.

SAMMY: So how could she come to you?

MICHAEL: I don't know. But she did.

(SAMMY feels MICHAEL's forehead.)

SAMMY: You remember Sigfried? Von Blaumstein? His woman came to him in the night, I remember him talking about it. A few weeks later he was dead.

MICHAEL: Sigfried?

SAMMY: Von Blaumstein. I remember him saying "Sammy, I'm thinking of going off the meat for awhile." A few weeks later his body was found dissolving into the floorboards, his flesh turned to goop.

MICHAEL: Where was this?

SAMMY: Outside Naples, after Napoleon, before Garibaldi. That's why we had to leave town. You don't remember any of this?

MICHAEL: Not clearly.

SAMMY: Well, it was a long time ago. Anyway, the peasants wanted to burn us after that. It was a long cart ride up to Rome, I can tell you that much.

MICHAEL: His woman came to him?

SAMMY: So he said, in a vision, late at night. I said he was dreaming, he said he wasn't, just like you. Helga. Blonde. Buxom.

Skin like cream, her hair in those rings they used to keep back then. In the end he just couldn't take it anymore.

(Sammy takes a long slurp, considering his friend.)

SAMMY: I need a cutter, Michael, a good cutter. If I'm going to bag for you I need to know you're going to be there.

MICHAEL: I'll be there, Sammy.

SAMMY: To cut them down, Michael.

MICHAEL: I'll be there.

SAMMY: Good. That's good. We'll be home one day, Michael, and when we are you'll be close to Maria again. As close as life will allow.

MICHAEL: Yes. As close as life will allow.

(Sammy takes out a small black book and consults it.)

SAMMY: Let's see . . . I have a woman, older but in excellent condition, met her at a pottery class, recently divorced. Hates Craig's List, loves Europeans. She might be something for next month.

MICHAEL: Excellent condition means she might not drink.

SAMMY: Good point. I'll check.

MICHAEL: What about the aerobics instructor you mentioned?

SAMMY: Out of town. I have a man—

MICHAEL: No men.

SAMMY: Men can be easy.

MICHAEL: For you, maybe, not for me.

SAMMY: You don't have to lie with them, Michael, just make small talk, just until the wine does its work.

MICHAEL: It is an abomination.

SAMMY: To make small talk?

MICHAEL: It is against Gott.

SAMMY: You know, Michael, the Bible is actually more progressive on these things than some would have us believe.

MICHAEL: I don't care about the Bible.

SAMMY: Michael, please, we are still Christians.

MICHAEL: NO MEN!

(beat)

They can smell it on me, the old ways. I'm uncomfortable, they're uncomfortable. They get anxious, I get anxious, and then all that fear goes into the meat.

SAMMY: It's not so easy, Michael, getting a woman.

MICHAEL: Was it ever easy?

SAMMY: Women are getting smarter, more independent. I can't just give them my googly eyes anymore, not like I used to.

MICHAEL: I have faith in you, Sammy.

SAMMY: Did you read the articles I sent you? More women have advanced degrees now than men, that's new.

MICHAEL: I read them.

(Sammy considers Michael unhappily, then returns to his book.)

SAMMY: Okay. I do have an ex-dancer, her flesh sculpted and engorged with training. She could be tasty.

MICHAEL: I wouldn't want to be a man today. All our natural instincts, our ancient privileges, reduced to a kind of crime. A kind of sickness.

SAMMY: In the West, maybe. Not in the East.

MICHAEL: Christendom is not what it used to be.

SAMMY: No.

MICHAEL: No.

(The two consider this. Then)

SAMMY: Give me a week. I'll find someone suitable.

MICHAEL: A week will be hard. I'll move what I have into the freezer until then.

SAMMY: You have a cuisinart?

MICHAEL: A cuisinart?

SAMMY: You know, for blending things.

MICHAEL: I have a blender. Why?

SAMMY: Make yourself a treat. You don't even need to thaw the meat, really, just put it in in little cubes.

MICHAEL: A treat?

SAMMY: A frozen treat, with lemon, orange juice, anything citrusy.

(He takes the lid off his frappe and shows it to Michael.)
It's great in the summer.

(Michael tries a slurp and smiles at his resourceful friend. They both laugh fairly mirthlessly for awhile as the lights fade.)

Information on this playwright may be found at www.smithandkraus.com. Click on the AUTHORS tab

Partial Objects

Sherry Kramer

Seriocomic
Paris, twenties.
Mephistopheles: The Devil, The Devil is ageless, naturally, but in this incarnation he is very hot in all senses of the word and could be nineteen or thirty-nine.

Partial Objects is an adaptation of Faust with two Fausts—a man and a woman. The scene happens the morning after Mephistopheles has spent the night seducing Paris, a befuddled everyman, giving him what feels like transcendent, perfect love. Eternally in despair since his expulsion from paradise, Mephistopheles is trying to find a way back into God's good graces. Now he must get Paris to promise his soul in return for a moment of true perfect love—not with Mephistopheles (it's worthless, in the scheme of things, with an angel) but with a mortal. Paris is both eager for this moment and tortured with jealousy. He doesn't want Mephistopheles to spend the night with anyone but him. Mephistopheles is both jaded beyond belief—he's been making this deal since the beginning of time—and eternally hopeful: Maybe this is the Faust who can have a moment of heaven on earth where it belongs and show God his father that the flesh is as sacred as the spirit. If this happens, the prodigal devil will have proved himself worthy of being reunited with his Father, and can return to his rightful place at God's side.

MEPHISTOPHELES: I don't know what all the fuss is all about. It's really very cut and dried.

PARIS: It's my soul. My soul!

MEPHISTOPHELES: Nonsense. Before I came you didn't think you had one.

PARIS: I don't see why you can't love me without it.

MEPHISTOPHELS: Who said anything about love?

PARIS: Let's go someplace, okay? Someplace where there aren't a lot of people. Morocco. Tahiti.

MEPHISTOPHELS: No more Morocco and no more Tahiti.

PARIS: Then how about my sister's house in Jersey? I haven't seen the new baby yet.

MEPHISTOPHELES: You really try my nerves. Why do you want to make me angry?

PARIS: I'm not the one who's trying to make anyone angry.

MEPHISTOPHELES: And I am?

PARIS: You have this thing about saying you love me.

MEPHISTOPHELES: It's not a thing about saying it. It's something I can't say.

PARIS: Yeah, yeah. Go ahead and hide behind an angel can't do this and that crap.

MEPHISTOPHELES: It is hardly crap.

PARIS: It is to me.

MEPHISTOPHELES: It wasn't last night.

PARIS: Stop talking to me about last night! I can't think about anything else! I've never been held like I was last night. What are you going to do about that! Tell me! What are you going to do about that!

MEPHISTOPHELES: I've already told you. Last night wasn't real.

PARIS: Don't do this to me!

MEPHISTOPHELES: Last night was an illusion.

PARIS: What are you talking about? The Great Wall, the Eiffel Tower, that—

MEPHISTOPHELES: All that you felt and all that you saw with me was mere illusion. You never left this room.

PARIS: But after, when you kissed me . . .

MEPHISTOPHELES: Apparition. Fantasy. Dream.

PARIS: I won't believe that!

MEPHISTOPHELES: Believe. I never touched you, or you me.

PARIS: You wanted me.

MEPHISTOPHELES: Someone had to hold your head down for you. Someone had to teach you how to pray.

PARIS: You liked it!

MEPHISTOPHELES: Liked it! I would love it, if I could. But you were made for love, not me.

PARIS: You're just a whore!

MEPHISTOPHELES: *(bows, elegantly)* For God, and no one else.

PARIS: You go to hell!!!

MEPHISTOPHELES: Been there. Done that. Listen. The moment for which you promised your soul will not be with me.

PARIS: Why not?

MEPHISTOPHELES: It will be with a woman.

PARIS: Who said anything about a woman?

MEPHISTOPHELES: You did, actually.

PARIS: When!

MEPHISTOPHELES: Last night. In the heat of passion. You called out a beautiful name.

PARIS: But I can't have it with anyone but you. It's not something that happens here.

MEPHISTOPHELES: You seem to think it did.

PARIS: That's different. It was with you.

MEPHISTOPHELES: With this woman it will be real.

PARIS: But I want you!

MEPHISTOPHELES: You want what you had last night.

PARIS: And why shouldn't I?

MEPHISTOPHELES: With this woman you will not have to share an illusion. You will have something real.

PARIS: *(laughing)* Real? You don't know the first thing about it. Last night was real.

MEPHISTOPHELES: With a woman, PARIS: , you can--

PARIS: Can what. WHAT! Look. Here's what happens with a woman. Here's what you think is real. I meet her. I wait for her to say she loves me. She says it. I look at her. I say to myself: "The rest of my life. Does this woman look like the rest of my life?" She doesn't. Or, it happens like this. I meet her. I wait for her to say she loves me. She doesn't. I realize I have to be the one who says it. I say it. Guess what happens next. Go on. Can't? After I say I love you I get to watch her look at me and say, to herself: "The rest of my life. Do I want this person to be my life for the rest of my life?" Last night was real.

MEPHISTOPHELES: Then one woman is like another to you, and it doesn't matter who I bring?

PARIS: No matter who you bring me, it will end the same.

MEPHISTOPHELES: You're sure?

PARIS: Are you asking me who I'd like? Because if you are, I'll tell you.

MEPHISTOPHELES: Who?

PARIS: Marilyn Monroe. Sorry.

MEPHISTOPHELES: *(a bit disgusted)* Yeah, I'll bet. I've someone else in mind for you.

PARIS: You do? Then why haven't you brought her here!

MEPHISTOPHELES: I will.

PARIS: When?

MEPHISTOPHELES: Soon.

PARIS: Why not now?

MEPHISTOPHELES: I must first show her what I've shown you.

PARIS: Oh. What do you mean . . . show her?

MEPHISTOPHELES: You know what I mean.

PARIS: Do you have to? I mean, isn't there some other way?

MEPHISTOPHELES: Not if she's to promise her soul.

PARIS: Well, what if she doesn't? What if she doesn't want to give you her soul?

MEPHISTOPHELES: You forget who you are talking to, Paris.

PARIS: Yeah, but if she doesn't want to I've given you my soul for nothing!

MEPHISTOPHELES: I will not take your soul until you've had the moment you've been promised. The two of you, together.

PARIS: But what if we can't?

MEPHISTOPHELES: The risk is mine.

PARIS: You're going to her tonight?

MEPHISTOPHELES: I am. It is time for the dream to end.
(He snaps his fingers. Paris falls immediately asleep, standing up.)
Sleep—and when you wake, say nothing of what has happened.
(Paris, sound asleep, backs into bed and lies down.)
Sleep.
(Gathering himself up for his dramatic exit.)
The day breaks. The night dies. And the Prince of Darkness flies.

*Information on this playwright may be found at
www.smithandkraus.com. Click on the AUTHORS tab*

Sex Lives of our Parents

Michael Mitnick

Comic
Jeff, twenties
Elliot, twenties

> *Jeff is engaged to Virginia who has begun to see visions of her mother's past. Jeff meets Elliot at a bar where Jeff relays his concerns and Elliot has some concerns of his own.*

JEFF: I caught her pouring cranberry juice into her Crispix. So I said, "Virginia, you poured cranberry juice into your Crispix." And she looks down into the bowl and it registers that she poured cranberry juice into her Crispix. So she dumps the whole thing into the garbage disposal, goes to the dish drainer, gets a new bowl, and I'm standing there grinding coffee right—

ELLIOT: Right.

JEFF: And the thing is going, "Vrrr, Vrrr, Vrrr, Vrrr."

ELLIOT: You can't hear her.

JEFF: Yeah. No. I mean, no I can't hear her. But that's not the point. The point is that I was distracted.

ELLIOT: Right.

JEFF: Right. So, "Vrrrr, Vrrrr, Vrrrr." And I look over at Virginia.

ELLIOT: And she's eating out of the garbage disposal?

JEFF: No—she's. Elliot. Stop guessing. I'm going to tell you. You don't have to guess.

ELLIOT: I was just trying to reciprocate. To show I'm listening.

JEFF: OK, but you also derailed the entire story.

ELLIOT: I'm sorry, Jeff.

ELLIOT looks off into the distance.

JEFF: It's not a big deal. I'm only—Elliot, are you crying?

ELLIOT: (He's not.) What? No.

JEFF: Um. So . . . Wait. What was I saying?

ELLIOT:	JEFF:
"V rrrr, Vrrrr, Vrrrr."	Right. Right. So I look back over

Elliot, Cranberry Juice? at her. And she's doing it

JEFF: In her Crispix. So I said, "Virginia, what are you thinking about?" And do you know what she said?

(Elliot starts to guess.)

Don't guess—I'm going to tell you. "I keep seeing my Mom with another man. He's older. And he's kissing her neck." "And this man begins to run his hands over her body."

(Elliot picks up his seltzer and drinks. He returns the drink to the table.)

ELLIOT: Wow. It's weird how her Mom doesn't stop with this guy if Virginia is standing there watching.

JEFF: No. She means she sees, like, visions. She thinks she sees visions of when her Mom was younger.

ELLIOT: That's messed up. That's like, um, Oedipus or Freud or something.

JEFF: Thanks for your diagnosis, Elliot.

ELLIOT: Yeah.

JEFF takes a sip of his beer. Why are these chairs so weird?

(Jeff is looking at someone in the bar.)

JEFF: Hey, you see her?

ELLIOT: Who? Her?

JEFF: Don't you dare point.

ELLIOT: I wasn't gonna point.

JEFF: You were gonna point.

ELLIOT: She's cute. Like pigtails.

JEFF: She keeps looking over here.

ELLIOT: Do you know her?

JEFF: I don't think so. How's Hannah?

ELLIOT: Good. Probably. She dumped me.

JEFF: What? When?

ELLIOT: Two nights ago. She told me she just wants to be my "friend." I told her I already have "friends." What I don't have is a girlfriend. She said that she . . . wanted to take some time off from dating. So she can focus on her custom jewelry business.

JEFF: I'm sorry, man. How long did you see her?

ELLIOT: Five months. Well . . . Like almost four months.She also got mad when I tried to guess what she was going to say next.

JEFF: I'm sorry, man.

ELLIOT: It's my lisp.

JEFF: It's not your lisp.

ELLIOT: It's my confidence.

JEFF: It might be your confidence.

(Elliot smiles a little.)

ELLIOT: Virginia has been acting weird at the gallery. I found her taking pictures of this dead mouse. Its head was halfway severed. Sort of disconnected. Didn't even get to eat the cheese. Virginia was kneeling and snapping photos' said something about Vanitas art.

JEFF: What's that?

ELLIOT: Jeff, what's wrong with me? Would you please just tell me? I feel like, like I've heard whispering behind my back my whole life.

JEFF: No one's whispering—

ELLIOT: Stop repeating back what I'm saying and just tell me. But it doesn't. It's like I'm trying to get to this mythical strip of land somewhere in the future. And no matter how fast and how far I run, it keeps getting further away.

JEFF: Farther. Farther away. Further.

JEFF shakes his head 'no.'

(silence)

You'll meet someone. I bet your future wife is somewhere eating a sandwich right now.

ELLIOT: Or getting fucked by another guy. I think you're only happy when I'm a mess.

(silence)

JEFF: Why does that girl keep looking over here? OK. You want to know?

ELLIOT: What?

JEFF: What's wrong with you. Do you actually want to know? You're depressed.

ELLIOT: So?

JEFF: So, it's depressing. Girls don't want to have to, like, jazz-i-fy your spirits every time they see you. Girls want to fall in love.

ELLIOT: I've got a lot to be depressed about. I don't have any money. I hate my job. I don't have a girlfriend. I don't have anything to look forward to. I was an alcoholic.

JEFF: But you shouldn't offer that information up front. I've heard you do it! "Hey, you're cute. I'm Elliot. I'm a recovering alcoholic. You look smart. Can I buy you a beer and wistfully watch you drink it?"

ELLIOT: I don't say that.

JEFF: Don't have any expectations. Just talk to her. Don't show you're interested. Just talk to her. And then, while you're talking, she'll be thinking, "Wait. Why isn't this guy hitting on me? Am I not as attractive as I thought? Do I have like boogers hanging out of my nose? Does he think I'm not good enough for him?"

ELLIOT: She will?

JEFF: Absolutely.

ELLIOT: Is that how you got Virginia?

JEFF: With Virginia I just knew. It was magical.

ELLIOT: No, man, you asked her out. I remember. She wore those green socks—

JEFF: Virginia's different. With her it was so easy. I just asked her out and she said, "Sure." And then marriage. Will you marry me? . . . "Sure." With Virginia it's just . . . easy. Easy.

(silence)

That girl is staring at you. Go introduce yourself.

ELLIOT: I don't like people I meet in bars.

JEFF: You're in a bar. C'mon. What do you have to lose?

ELLIOT: It's true. Hell, I could even make another friend.

(Elliot takes a sip of seltzer.)

Is it just me or is this chair like super weird?

(Jeff kicks the bottom of Elliot seat.)

Stop it.

(He kicks the bottom of Elliot's seat again. Elliot turns and kicks Jeff's seat. Jeff kicks Elliot's seat harder and harder. Elliot stands up. He's terribly nervous)

Fine!

JEFF: Wipe the sweat off your upper lip. Fix your hair.

ELLIOT: What's wrong with it?

JEFF: It just . . . I dunno. Just like, move it around.

ELLIOT: Like this?

JEFF: Yeah . . . . .I guess. And unbutton your shirt a button.

(He does.)

No, not from the bottom. The top button. Unbutton that.

(He does.)

ELLIOT: Do I look OK?

JEFF: Yeah. You look good. And remember . . . she's looking for someone too. You're not trying to trick her. Elliot. You're a great guy.

ELLIOT: Can I hug you?

JEFF: . . . ehhhhh . . . fine.

(They hug. Over Elliot's shoulder, Jeff sees something.)

Elliot!! Um . . . behind. Ah shit. Behind. Um. Behind that girl I just saw Hannah.

ELLIOT: What?? She's here? I should go talk to her.

(Elliot re-buttons his top button, frantically.)

JEFF: No, man. She's . . .

(Elliot is craning his neck. He takes a step back, heart-broken.)

ELLIOT: Who's that guy? I've never seen that guy before. Who's that guy? And why is she making out with him?

JEFF: She looks . . . drunk.

ELLIOT: She never kissed me in public. Said PDA made her want to vomit.

JEFF: Maybe she'll vomit in his mouth. Or his ear. Or his . . . wow. They're really going at it.

(Both their heads rotate to the side, following the 'action.')

Uh . . . Listen man, you still should go talk to that other girl.

ELLIOT: I need to leave.

JEFF: Elliot . . .

ELLIOT: Can we go please?

JEFF: I still have half my . . . Yeah, man. No problem.

Information on this playwright may be found at www.smithandkraus.com. Click on the AUTHORS tab

When January Feels Like Summer

Cori Thomas

Seriocomic
Devaun, nineteen, African American
Jeron, eighteen, African American

Devaun and Jeron are riding the subway together. Devaun tells Jeron about a troubling encounter he had with a man in the neighborhood named Lorrance (pronounced "Lorrhans"—French prononciation).

On the train, Devaun and Jeron sit.

DEVAUN: *(lowering his voice slightly and looking around to see he cannot be heard)* Yo, Jeron, yo yo, you know that dude Lorrance?

JERON: Who?

DEVAUN: Lorrance man, you know Lorrance, tall skinny brotha. Look like one a them lollipops. He got his hair comb back. Look like he got a relaxer.

JERON: No man, auno know who that is? Whachu mean by he look like a lollipop?

DEVAUN: Them pops they sell for ten cents at Bodega La Sala?

JERON: What? Whachu talkin' bout, fool?

DEVAUN: Not the round ones, those is 5 cent, these is long and twisted around, maybe two inches long. Ten cent. It got stripes, look like they going down around to the stick. It can almost seem like they twirlin'.

JERON: What, man, WHAT?!

DEVAUN: They come in all the flavors, in stripes. The stripes look like they goin' down the stick in a circle.

JERON: Yeh, yeh, yeh, hold up, you talkin' bout a dude always got a bow tie on. He tall and got a long skinny head with greasy hair might be jerri curl.

DEVAUN: That's Lorrance, man.

JERON: I know who you mean now, yeh, yeh, yeh.

DEVAUN: Lorrance.

JERON: He wear purple suits and shoes and socks to match it and big wide hats look like they Mexican or Greek.

DEVAUN: Yeh, yeh, tha's him. I think he gay.

JERON: For his sake, I hope so. Dressed the way he is? And he got them big white womanly sunglasses with diamond initials in the corner.

DEVAUN: He gon put his hand on my shoulder yesterday just as I was reachin' for a Pepsi, man.

JERON: Yo, yo, yo Devaun, whatchu talkin' bout? What he put his hand on you for?

DEVAUN: Auno. He come up behind me, and got the nerve to put his hand on my shoulder, then talkin' bout (imitating Lorrance) "How bout it?"

JERON: He say that?

(he cracks up.)

Don't make me laugh Devaun. He ain't say that. Tell me he ain't say that to you.

DEVAUN: You got my word. I swear it on the bible. I swear it on two bibles. I is just mindin' my own business tryin' to find the coldest Pepsi, 'cause you got to reach way in the back to get the cold ones, and dude step right behind me with his hand, got his glasses on too, touch my shoulder and say in a low quiet voice, "How about it." Dude gotta nerve to try and homosex me right out in the public eye and what have you?

JERON: So what did you say to that fool?

DEVAUN: I turn to him and I say "Lorrance, you better take yo skank hand off me." He take his hand back quick. Like this.

(shows him)

Like he touch something hot. Then his mouth drop open, like this.

(shows him)

Then I bump him with my shoulder hard and said, "You betta fuckin stay the fuck away from me you fuckin fuck-head. I will fuck you the fuck up, if you don't fuck the fuck off fuckhead!"

JERON: Damn! So then what did he say?

DEVAUN: He ain't say nothin'. Just look at me with his eyes and mouth

(shows him)
Like this.

JERON: You ain't serious.

DEVAUN: I'm serial. In the sto, man. Only reason I didn't kill that fool is he go to the same church as my Moms.

JERON: Yeh, yeh, I hear you. But wait, wait, hold up, suppose the dude, Lorrance, suppose he was just trying to christianize you. He religious. I know you seen him singing them hymns in the street on Sundays, loud and all outta tune and shit. That shit hurt your ears.

DEVAUN: Yeh, I seen and heard him. But Jeron, belee me, that ain't it.

JERON: Dude might have HIV, Shit, Her P E's! All them initials.

DEVAUN: Damn, I ain't even thought about that. Damn!

JERON: Suppose he stop just touchin' people on the shoulder and instead start layin' in wait to pounce and infest himself on women and children, man. This here some incredulous shit we dealin' with.

DEVAUN: Wait a minute Jeron, hold up, he ain't gon be messing with women if he gay.

JERON: You got a point. Still though, I hope he don't come trying to touch on me. Damn!

DEVAUN: I didn't like him to have the nerve to be tryin' to propose his shit to me without my expressive invitation. I a man, he a man too. My cousin gay and we except his ass and respectfullin' him how he is. But he don't just go and start feelin' on people less he know first they be the same way. That tell you something important about this situation. But I think the women is safe.

JERON: Well, boys and men ain't safe. How about they sorry ass?

DEVAUN: It's clear to me this fool was tryin' to homosex me in the Bodega La Sala while I was in the innocental act of my gettin' my cold Pepsi.

JERON: I'm tryin' to comprehend the magnitude of the situation . . . You sho that's all the dude said?

DEVAUN: I think so, but truth is I was shockified. And I was thinkin' about the innocental children of the world. Them kids man, them kids. He had a strange look in his eye, Lorrance. Made the blood in my heart curdle up. I went home and told my Moms, and she said we should pray for him

DEVAUN: *(cont.)* 'cause maybe he lost sight of the flock.

JERON: What that mean?

DEVAUN: It's religious.

JERON: You ever seen that bow tie he wear, it look like it from the olden days?

DEVAUN: Dude gotta be thirty at least.

JERON: That man at least thirty, man. He mature. He wear them wide pants with the cuff at the bottom. He at least thirty, maybe forty.

DEVAUN: Why he gon pick me? Everyone man, everyone know I got to get with my woman every day, sometimes two or three times a day even.

JERON: Two or three times a day, I know you exaggeratin' Devaun.

DEVAUN: Man, I go see Lakwanda, and if she not there or she busy, I get wit Doreen. You seen Doreen since she lost that weight? She look sweet man, real sweet.

JERON: Yeh, she look nice. She look real nice, Jamal say he gon get wit her.

DEVAUN: He better stay away from her. She ain't no free agent.

JERON: Yo, yo, yo, you can't be greedy, Devaun, keepin' them two or three women outta circulation just for your own convenience. You got all them women hooked up witchu. How you do that? You should be spreadin' that shit around equanimibly, man.

DEVAUN: *(lowering his voice)* Jeron, this Lorrance thing has mess me up. I keep thinking about it.

JERON: Aiigt, well, you need to speak directly and explicitly to the dude and warn him he playin' with hot fire. You got to be real firm wit people like that. You got to tell him to never put his hand on no one no more.
(getting loud)
Not just you, nobody in the world. Tell him, "This is the United States of America, and people not

JERON: *(cont.)* supposed to do that shit here." If he want to start his homosexual bizness with people you gotta go warn people about that shit. It's your duty, man. You gotta set the example. Cause like you say, innocent children is walking around. They's easy prey, man. Suppose he try somethin' with them next? That's on you. You need to start warnin' these people's ass around here.

DEVAUN: When?

JERON: Auno. Tomorrow. After we get off from work.

DEVAUN: Yeh, yeh, no no, when you right, you right.

Information on this playwright may be found at www.smithandkraus.com. Click on the AUTHORS tab

WILD ANIMALS YOU SHOULD KNOW

Thomas Higgins

Dramatic
Matthew and Jacob, both teens

> *Matthew and Jacob are friends. Actually, Matthew is Jacob's only friend, as he's sort of a weenie. Both are in the Boy Scouts. They are spying on their scoutmaster, Rodney. They think he's in his house having sex with another man.*

> *In the backyard. Matthew and Jacob lay on their stomachs, in sleeping bags, on the lawn. They both have binoculars up to their faces.*

MATTHEW: See anything?

JACOB: Nope.

MATTHEW: Shit, where do you think he is?

JACOB: I don't know; you saw him.

MATTHEW: Damnit. I can't believe he's not bangin' some dude again.

JACOB: You're sure it was him?

MATTHEW: Yep; positive.

JACOB: Scoutmaster Rodney.

MATTHEW: Dude, I swear.

JACOB: Which house was it?

MATTHEW: That one, over there.

JACOB: Alright.

MATTHEW: You stay on that one; I'll check the others.

JACOB: Why would you check the others?

MATTHEW: To see if he's banging someone else.

JACOB: Why would he be banging someone—?

MATTHEW: I dunno; aren't you guys all transient and whatnot?

JACOB: I'm going to pretend I didn't hear that.

MATTHEW: Just look alright?

They do; JACOB eventually gives up.

JACOB: Oh, hey: so what's your Eagle project gonna be?

MATTHEW: Huh?

JACOB: Your community service project—the last big thing? What's your plan?

MATTHEW: Probably just wing it.

JACOB: What? You can't . . . wing it. It's like a big deal. And it has to be approved, and everything.

MATTHEW: So?

JACOB: So: you better come up with one fast.

MATTHEW: What's yours?

JACOB: I'm gonna plant a vegetable garden where the old strip mall used to be.

MATTHEW: Gay.

JACOB: What? It's agro-conscious.

MATTHEW: Gay.

JACOB: Yeah, well, we can smell our own, right?
(Matthew punches him hard in the arm.)

JACOB: Ow! What the hell?

MATTHEW: I am not gay.
(beat)
You just give really good head.

JACOB: You wish. God.
(Jacob rubs his arm.)

JACOB: Sometimes I seriously wonder why we're friends.

MATTHEW: Because you're in love with me.

JACOB: I am not.

MATTHEW: And I don't reciprocate it. Which makes you not only a homosexual—

JACOB: Duh.

MATTHEW: But, like, a masochist.

JACOB: Am not!

MATTHEW: No? How's your arm?
(Jacob stops rubbing it.)

JACOB: So, what does that make you?

MATTHEW: I dunno. A narcissist, I guess.
(a shrug)
I'm not gay, I just want everyone to want me.

JACOB: And how does your girlfriend feel about that?

MATTHEW: Who knows? She's Becky; she's prude as hell. I'm beginning to think she doesn't feel anything.

JACOB: Uh-huh.

MATTHEW: She finally let me touch her boobs.

JACOB: Gross.

MATTHEW: I think it was a big step, though. I think it like really meant something . . . for her.

(Jacob can't help but laugh.)

JACOB: God, you're terrible.

MATTHEW: Yeah, yeah.

JACOB: You really are.

(Matthew gives up on his binoculars, wanders . . .)

MATTHEW: Ugh.

JACOB: What?

MATTHEW: I'm just sick of this. I'm sick of knowing what's gonna happen, you know? Like, tonight: be prepared. What is that?

JACOB: Um, the boy scout motto?

MATTHEW: Right, but like . . . you know what? Being prepared sucks. It's goddamn predictable.

JACOB: . . . okay.

MATTHEW: I know I'll finish this year high honors; I know that I'll letter next year in soccer; I know I'll already be in the running for valedictorian—

JACOB: Not if I can help it.

MATTHEW: And I know all of this makes my parents happy; which keeps them out of my hair; so that I can do . . . what? I am capable of these things, but none of them feel like they're mine, you know? Where's the challenge in that?

JACOB: Well, your ego is definitely yours.

MATTHEW: It's not ego, it's what will be. I am constantly fighting not to be a spectator of myself. Do you have any idea what that's like?

JACOB: Not really, no.

MATTHEW: I mean, don't you ever want to do something just because you can?

JACOB: Um . . .

MATTHEW: Just because it's possible?

JACOB: . . . sometimes.

MATTHEW: Don't you ever wanna just, like, go crazy? Just to, you know . . . feel?

JACOB: I guess.

MATTHEW: Anything?

JACOB: Maybe.

MATTHEW: Well, right. Okay, then!

JACOB: Okay.

MATTHEW: So, yes! Let's do something crazy!

JACOB: Let's do it.

(Jacob leans in and plants a big kiss on Matthew. Matthew shoves him off.)

MATTHEW: Dude, what the hell?!

JACOB: What, I—?

MATTHEW: What the hell, man!

JACOB: I thought you meant . . .

MATTHEW: No! I didn't!

JACOB: Really?

MATTHEW: I was gonna say let's jump off the roof!

JACOB: Oh.

MATTHEW: Or like egg the neighbor's house! Jesus, Jacob.

JACOB: I'm sorry.

MATTHEW: Goddamnit.

(Matthew shakes his head—he's less bothered by the actual kiss than he is by the "burden" of it.)

JACOB: I'm sorry, Matthew.

MATTHEW: It's fine. Let's just . . . it's fine. Fuck.

JACOB: I'm sorry.

MATTHEW: Let's just look at the fucking stars or something.

(He rolls over on his back. JACOB eventually does the same, rubs his arm.)

MATTHEW: Does it hurt?

JACOB: . . . no.

(beat)

MATTHEW: Are you pouting now?

JACOB: No.

(beat)

MATTHEW: Wanna see who can pitch a tent faster?

JACOB: What? No. Fuck you.

(Matthew starts stroking himself inside his sleeping bag.)

MATTHEW: I'm totally gonna win . . .

(Jacob eventually caves, starts stroking himself too—and somehow their strangely playful, homo-erotic balance has been restored . . . for now.)

Information on this playwright may be found at www.smithandkraus.com. Click on the AUTHORS tab

Rights & Permissions

The entire text of each play may be obtained by contacting the rights holder.

Monologues

DARKPOOL © 2010 by Don Nigro. Reprinted by permission of Don Nigro. For performance rights, contact Samuel French, Inc. (www.samuelfrench.com) 212-206-8990.

DON GIOVANNI © 2009 by Don Nigro. Reprinted by permission of Don Nigro. For performance rights, contact Samuel French, Inc. (www.samuelfrench.com) 212-206-8990.

FIRST DAY OF SCHOOL © 2010 by Billy Aronson. Reprinted by permission of Billy Aronson. For performance rights, contact Broadway Play Publishing, 224 E. 62nd St New York, NY 10065 (www.broadwayplaypubl.com) 212-772-8334.

FLESH AND THE DESERT © 2012 by Carson Kreitzer. Reprinted by permission of Bruce Ostler/Mark Orsini, Bret Adams Ltd. For performance rights, contact Bruce Ostler (bostler@bretadamsltd.net) or Mark Orsini (morsini@bretadamsltd.net).

HURT VILLAGE © 2012 by Katori Hall. Reprinted by permission of Olivier Sultan, Creative Artists Agency. performance rights are handled by Dramatists Play Service, 440 Park Ave. S., New York, NY 10016. 212-683-8960. (www.dramatists.com).

I COULD NEVER LIVE HERE © 2011 by C.S. Hanson. Reprinted by permission of the author. For performance rights, contact C.S. Hanson (cshansonplays@yahoo.com).

I KNOW © 2011 by Jacquelyn Reingold. Reprinted by permission of Jacquelyn Reingold. For performance rights, contact Jacquelyn Reingold (jackierein@verizon.net).

THE INVITATION © 2008 by Brian Parks. Reprinted by permission of Brian Parks. The entire text is published by NY Theatre Experience (www.nytheatre.com) in Plays and Playwrights 2010. For performance rights, contact Brian Parks (bparks3000@yahoo.com).

JEROME VIA SATELLITE (from THE SPIN CYCLE) © 2009 by Jerrod Bogard . Reprinted by permission of Jerrod Bogard. The entire text is published by NY Theatre Experience (www. nytheatre.com) in Plays and Playwrights 2010. For performance rights, contact Jerrod Bogard (jerrodbogard@gmail.com).

JUST YOUR AVERAGE G.I. JOE (from THE SPIN CYCLE) © 2006 by Jerrod Bogard. Reprinted by permission of Jerrod Bogard. Published by NY Theatre Experience(www.nytheatre.com) in Plays and Playwrights 2010. For performance rights, contact Jerrod Bogard (jerrodbogard@gmail.com).

KIN © 2011 by Bathsheba Doran. Reprinted by permission of Mark Subias. For performance rights, contact Dramatists Play Service, 440 Park Ave. S, New York, NY 10016 (www. dramatists.com) (212-683-8960).

LOOKING AGAIN © 2011 by Charles Evered. Reprinted by permission of Susan Gurman, Susan Gurman Agency. For performance rights, contact For performance rights, contact Susan Gurman (susan@gurmanagency.com)

THE MOTHERFU**ER WITH THE HAT © 2011 by Stephen Adly Guirgis. Reprinted by permission of John Buzzetti, William Morris Endeavor Entertainment. For performance rights, contact Dramatists Play Service, 440 Park Ave. S., New York, NY 10016 (www.dramatists.com) (212-683-8960).

THE MOUNTAINTOP © 2011 by Katori Hall. Reprinted by permission of the author. For performance rights, contact Dramatists Play Service, 440 Park Ave. S., New York, NY 10016 (www.dramatists.com) (212-683-8960).

MURPH © 2011 by Catherine M. O'Neill. Reprinted by permission of the author. For performance rights, contact Catherine M. O'Neill (coneill2@lesley.edu).

THE NAVIGATOR © 2008 by Eddie Antar. Reprinted by permission of the author. For performance rights, contact Eddie Antar (eantar@nyc.rr.com). The entire text has been published by Smith and Kraus, Inc. in *New Playwrights: The Best Plays of 2012.*

PARAFFIN—from THE HALLWAY TRILOGY © 2011 by Adam Rapp. Reprinted by permission of Mark Subias. Published by Theatre Communications Group. For performance rights, contact Mark Subias (mark@marksubias.com).

PASTIME © 2011 by Greg Owens. Reprinted by permission of Greg Owens. For performance rights, contact Broadway Play Publishing, 224 E. 62nd St New York, NY 10065 (www.broadwayplaypubl.com) 212-772-8334.

THE RELEASE OF A LIVE PERFORMANCE © 2010 by Sherry Kramer. Reprinted by permission of Morgan Jenness, Abrams Artists Agency. For performance rights, contact Broadway Play Publishing, 224 E. 62nd St New York, NY 10065 (www.broadwayplaypubl.com) 212-772-8334.

ROGER AND VANESSA © 2010 by Brett C. Leonard. Reprinted by permission of Brett C. Leonard. For performance rights, contact Broadway Play Publishing, 224 E. 62nd St New York, NY 10065 (www.broadwayplaypubl.com) 212-772-8334.

ROSE—from THE HALLWAY TRILOGY © 2011 by Adam Rapp. Reprinted by permission of Mark Subias. Published by Theatre Communications Group. For performance rights, contact Mark Subias (mark@marksubias.com).

ROW AFTER ROW © 2011 by Jessica Dickey. Reprinted by permission of Morgan Jenness, Abrams Artists Agency. For performance rights, contact Morgan Jenness (morgan.jenness@abramsartny.com).

WAITING FOR WEINSTEIN © 2011 by Bob Lundin. Reprinted by permission of Robert Lundin. For performance rights, contact Robert Lundin(rklundin@aol.com).

WHEN JANUARY FEELS LIKE SUMMER © 2011 by Cori Thomas. Reprinted by permission of Ron Gwiazda, Abrams Artists Agency. For performance rights, contact Ron Gwiazda (ron.gwiazda@abramsartny.com.

WILD ANIMALS YOU SHOULD KNOW © 2011 by Thomas Higgins. Reprinted by permission of Patrick Herold, International Creative Management. For performance rights, contact Patrick Herold pherold@icmpartners.com).

WOOF © 2009 by Y York. Reprinted by permission of Bruce Ostler/Mark Orsini, Bret Adams Ltd.. For performance rights, contact Broadway Play Publishing, 224 E. 62nd St New York, NY 10065 (www.broadwayplaypubl.com) 212-772-8334.

Scenes

AFTER © 2011 by Chad Beckim. Reprinted by permission of Mark Armstrong, Paradigm Agency. For performance rights, contact Samuel French, Inc. (www.samuelfrench.com) (212-206-8990).

ASUNCION © 2011 by Jesse Eisenberg. Reprinted by permission of Joanne Wiles, International Creative Management. For performance rights, contact Joanne Wiles (jwiles@icmpartners.com).

BLOOD AND GIFTS © 2010 by J.T. Rogers. Reprinted by permission of Victoria Fox, Faber and Faber, Inc., an affiliate of Farrar, Straus & Giroux, LLC. For performance rights, contact Dramatists Play Service, 440 Park Ave. S., New York, NY 10016 (www.dramatists.com) 212-683-8960.